GENESIS

BRINGING THE BIBLE TO LIFE

Genesis, by John H. Walton, Janet Nygren, and Karen H. Jobes
(12 sessions)

Esther, by Karen H. Jobes and Janet Nygren
(8 sessions)

John, by Gary M. Burge, Karen Lee-Thorp, and Karen H. Jobes
(12 sessions)

Romans, by Douglas J. Moo, Karen Lee-Thorp, and Karen H. Jobes
(12 sessions)

Ephesians, by Klyne Snodgrass, Karen Lee-Thorp, and Karen H. Jobes
(6 sessions)

Hebrews, by George H. Guthrie, Janet Nygren, and Karen H. Jobes
(8 sessions)

GENESIS

The Covenant Comes to Life

John H. Walton

Janet Nygren

Series Editor, Karen H. Jobes

BRINGING
THE
BIBLE
TO LIFE

ZONDERVAN®

ZONDERVAN.com/
AUTHORTRACKER
follow your favorite authors

ZONDERVAN®

Bringing the Bible to Life: Genesis
Copyright © 2008 by John H. Walton, Janet Nygren, and Karen H. Jobes

ISBN 978-0-310-27648-7

Interior design by Michelle Espinoza

Printed in the United States of America

08 09 10 11 12 13 14 • 23 22 21 20 19 18 17 16 15 14 13 12 11 10 9 8 7 6 5 4 3 2 1

CONTENTS

SERIES PREFACE

Have you ever been in a small-group Bible study where the leader read a passage from the Bible and then invited the members of the group to share what the passage meant to them? God wants to speak to each person individually through the Bible, but such an approach to group study can often be a frustrating and shallow experience for both leader and participants. And while the same passage can speak in various ways into people's lives, the meat of the Word is found in what the biblical writer intended to say about God and our relationship to him. The Bringing the Bible to Life series is for those who are ready to move from a surface reading of the Bible into a deeper understanding of God's Word.

But the Bible, though perhaps familiar, was written in ancient languages and in times quite different from our own, so most readers need a bit more help getting to a deeper understanding of its message. A study that begins and ends with what a passage "means to me" leaves the meaning of the passage unanchored and adrift in the thoughts—and perhaps the misunderstanding—of the reader. But who has time to delve into the history, language, cultures, and theology of the Bible? That's the work of biblical scholars who spend their lives researching, teaching, and writing about the ancient Scriptures. The need is to get the fruit of all that research into the hands of those in small-group Bible studies.

Zondervan's NIV Application Commentary (NIVAC) series was written to bring the best of evangelical biblical scholarship to those who want to know *both* the historical meaning of the biblical text *and* its contemporary significance. This companion series, Bringing the Bible to Life, is intended to bring that material into small-group studies in an easy-to-use format. Pastors, Christian education teachers, and small-group leaders whether in church, campus, or home settings will find these guides to be an enriching resource.

Each guide in the series provides an introduction to the biblical book that concisely summarizes the background information needed to better understand the original historical context. Six to twelve sessions per guide, with each session consisting of eleven to twelve discussion questions, allow a focused study that moves beyond superficial Bible reading. Relevant excerpts from the corresponding NIVAC commentary provide easy access into additional material for those interested in going even deeper. A closing section in each session assists the group in responding to God's Word together or individually. Guidance for leading each session is included, making the task of small-group leadership more manageable for busy lives.

If you want to move from the biblical text to contemporary life on solid ground, this series has been written for you.

Karen H. Jobes, PhD
Gerald F. Hawthorne Professor of
New Testament Greek and Exegesis
Wheaton College and Graduate School

OF SPECIAL NOTE

Your experience with and understanding of the book of Genesis can be deepened and enriched by referring to the volume on which it is based: *The NIV Application Commentary: Genesis* by John H. Walton, published by Zondervan in 2001.

INTRODUCTION[1]

How can a document that was written thousands of years ago in another language, to a cultural group that bears virtually no similarity to our own, have any relevance to us? The lessons of Genesis are rich and broad, but we need to proceed very carefully so that we don't end up with what *we* want Genesis to say instead of the message *God* intends us to have. If any culture at any time could ask any question of Genesis and come up with its own answers, the message of the book would be in constant flux. Our goal is to understand as best we can what Genesis meant to the people when it was originally written, how it fits with God's overall message of the Bible, and then to look at concepts that specifically translate to our times.

Tradition attributes the authorship of Genesis to Moses, although the book makes no claim of its own. It's not out of the question that others contributed to the work, but we accept the inspiration, purpose, and creative mind behind it to be Moses (inspired, of course, by God himself). His audience was the Israelites, sometime between their departure from slavery in Egypt and their entrance into the Promised Land. Genesis reveals the nature of the God they belong to, and helps them to understand who they are as a people, a people distinct from the other nations that face them.

In order to understand Genesis, then, we have to do our best to get into the world of Moses and the people he served. What was important to them? How did they think about life and God? How were they influenced by the cultures around them? What needs or fears of the people was Moses responding to? The expertise of John Walton will help us as we go through each lesson, but it's important for you, the modern reader, to put aside some of your preconceived notions temporarily.

By way of example—creation. Since there were no evolutionary theories floating around then that Moses may have been trying to counter, there must have been another purpose to Genesis 1. The mythology of Near Eastern cultures is actually a lot more relevant. That's not to say that Genesis is a myth. But the literary similarities between Genesis and the myths of the Near East give us a window into the thinking of that time and help us understand what made the God of the Israelites distinct from the gods of other people. Another example—Abraham pretends his wife, Sarah, is his sister. We could think of all sorts of family therapy they might need, but we actually have no idea what cultural relevance that incident had back then. Can we leave it aside and look for other things that tie those chapters together?

What is much more important is God's revelation of himself to humanity. Genesis is the beginning of God's story. The climax of God's story comes when he sends his son Jesus to the world he made, so that we get the fullest picture possible of what God is like and what the ideal person is like. But the world wasn't ready for that yet. We begin where God wants us to begin—his masterful creation, understood from the perspective of an Israelite wandering in the desert. Also important is the nature of humanity and its bent toward sin. God quickly turns his attention to one nation so that he can reveal himself more fully to them, and then bless others through them. So his covenant with Israel is of critical importance as it develops through Genesis.

It is admittedly ambitious to cover all of Genesis in twelve sessions, but this will allow you to see the big picture and major themes without getting too caught up in the details. It will require reading significant chunks of Genesis at times—but fortunately Genesis consists mainly of storytelling, which makes it easier to read at length. Feel free to tailor your study as necessary—each session is subdivided if you want to take it at a slower pace. The hope is that you enjoy Genesis, leading you to glorify God all the more by enjoying what you learn about him.

NOTE

1. This introduction is based on *The NIV Application Commentary: Genesis* (hereafter referred to as *NIVAC: Genesis*) by John H. Walton (Grand Rapids, Mich.: Zondervan, 2001), 19–56.

CREATION

Genesis 1:1–2:3

Most of us have some familiarity with Genesis 1 and the many hot debates that go along with it: creationism versus evolution, the question of the twenty-four-hour days of creation, the age of the earth — in general, how literally are we to understand this first book of the Bible? But think about it — many of the questions we try to answer looking at Genesis 1 were probably not on the minds of the original audience. The existence of God wasn't an issue — but rather, how many gods were there and who controlled what? What is the sun made of was much less important than will it rain on our crops and will we survive the next storm? Our questions today are the result of the most recent centuries of thinking framed by the scientific process — getting to the bottom of how things work. Instead of jumping into the modern debate, we're going to start by trying to put ourselves in the shoes of the Israelites who first heard this creation account, and think about the beginning from their point of view.

IN THE BEGINNING[1]

Read Genesis 1:1–5.

1. Many conservative scholars are in general agreement that Moses was the principal, if not the only, author of Genesis.[2] In that case, the first audience would have been the Israelites before they settled in the Promised Land. Thinking about their roots, and where they had been for hundreds of years in slavery, what cultural backgrounds were they most likely to be familiar with? What sorts of issues might they face in the wilderness for which they would turn to God for answers?

2. When *we* think about creation, our minds immediately jump to the origin of matter. What do John 1:3, Colossians 1:16–17, and Hebrews 11:3 say about God's role in creation? How does Romans 1:18–20 view this?

GOING DEEPER

We live in a world far different from the world of the Old Testament. We must recognize the elements that distinguish these two worlds and make appropriate adjustments to our expectations. In our world, we believe reality is described most accurately in scientific terms. Mythology in the ancient world played the role that science plays in our modern world — it contained the explanation of how the world came into being and how it worked.[3]

3. Comparing the beginning of Genesis to mythology does not make the creation story a myth, but rather gives us a window into the culture of that time. Mythology in the ancient Near East suggests the beginning as a period of chaos and darkness, with the elements themselves gradually taking on names and powers to explain the existence of forces familiar to everyone. For example, in Mesopotamia, the wind was understood to disrupt the waters and the waters became known by the name Tiamat — the goddess of the ocean.[4] How do the first two verses of Genesis coincide with this description of ancient Near East mythology? How are they different?

4. If we try to understand the creation from a scientific perspective, the separation of light and darkness (causing day and night on the first day) sets us up for confusion when we compare it to God's creative acts on the fourth day (Gen. 1:14–19). This was not likely an issue for the original audience because they were not concerned about the mechanics. It's a lot more helpful to think about creation as an organizing process — creating roles and functions for each part of the cosmos.[5] How does the creation of day and night bring order out of a formless and empty darkness?

ORGANIZING THE EARTH[6]

Read Genesis 1:6–13.

5. It's not too hard to begin to see a pattern as God continues to create on subsequent days. What things do you find in common in the accounts for the second and third days of creation? What do these tell you about God?

GOING DEEPER

The initial verses we have studied reveal that God alone takes responsibility for imposing order on chaos. He demonstrates his power and sovereignty by bringing the cosmos into conformity with his purposes. He does not accomplish this through battle with cosmic monsters, as the rest of the ancient world portrayed it, but by simply speaking the functions into existence.[7]

6. Try to think like an ancient Israelite now—that is, don't think about the structures that are being formed, but think about the functions of the things that are talked about in days two and three. How would you describe what is being formed on these days, and what importance would they have for you in the kind of life you live?

7. God created a world that could provide for its inhabitants and called it good. Think about the Israelites' fight for survival. Do you think they thought all of creation was good? Why or why not? Is our perspective today any different? What does it teach us about our relationship to God?

FILLING THE EARTH[8]

Read Genesis 1:14–31.

8. When I prepare my garden in the spring, I have to think things through pretty carefully—both the order and the space I have. I can't plant seeds before I've prepared the soil properly, and I've got to make sure I've left enough room for young plants to look just right when they fill out and bloom. If you line up day one with day four, two with five, and three with six, what do you notice about God's planning and ordering of creation?

9. We often think of people as God's crowning touch to creation, made, as 1:26–27 describes, in God's image to rule the earth. In some ways, our culture exploits that belief; in other ways, it denies the significance of it. How do you see this working itself out in today's world? What do you suppose God's intention was?

GOING DEEPER

In the ancient worldview people were slaves to the gods with no dignity other than that which came from the knowledge that the gods could not get along without humans to meet their needs. Whereas Mesopotamian literature is concerned about the jurisdiction of the various gods in the cosmos with humankind at the bottom of the heap, the Genesis account is interested in the jurisdiction of human-kind over the rest of creation as a result of the image of God in which people were created. In the biblical view, it is the concept of being in the image of God that provides for human dignity and the sanctity of human life.[9]

10. One other aspect of filling the earth, of course, is the well-known phrase to "be fruitful and multiply." However, this should be seen not as a command, but a blessing. For, "[i]n the ancient world, the ability to reproduce was seen as a gift from God."[10]

The language throughout Genesis reflects this, and God's blessing is particularly evident in the genealogies. How does the gift of fruitfulness, together with the mission to subdue and rule the world, reflect the image of God as Creator?

A DAY OF REST[11]

Read Genesis 2:1–3.

GOING DEEPER

This seventh day is not a theological appendix to the creation account, just to bring closure now that the main event of creating people has been reported. It intimates the purpose of creation and of the cosmos. God not only sets up the cosmos so that people will have a place; he also sets up the cosmos to serve as his temple. As Wenham[12] observes, the creation of people may be the climax of the six days of work, but it is not the conclusion of the narrative. It is the seventh day that is blessed and sanctified, which suggests the significance of what happens there.[13]

11. Ancient Near East mythology talks about gods creating resting places for themselves, which are their temples, and also equates their temples with the cosmos. Look at Isaiah 66:1, Psalm 132:13 – 14, and Psalm 104:2 – 4. How does Scripture expand on this idea? How does Jesus confirm this as described in Hebrews 8:1 – 6? What does this say about "our" world?

12. The idea of "entering God's rest" (Heb. 4:1) has generally appealed to me in the form of imitating God by ceasing work and putting my feet up on a Sunday afternoon after church. In light of the last question, however, I think entering into the holy, royal throne room of God is more of what Scripture has in mind. How does your celebration of the Sabbath reflect the privilege of entering into the presence of our Creator and honoring him as the ruler of the cosmos?

RESPONDING TO GOD'S WORD

IN YOUR GROUP:

It seems fitting to end this study of creation with a song of praise for the Creator. The hymn "How Great Thou Art" was written in 1885 by Carl Gustav Boberg in Sweden and translated into English by Stuart Hine.[14] Depending on your group, find a recording to sing along to, or sing *a cappella* with all your heart.

O Lord my God! When I in awesome wonder, consider all the works Thy
hands have made.

I see the stars, I hear the mighty thunder, Thy power throughout the universe
displayed.

Refrain:

Then sings my soul, my Savior God, to Thee; how great Thou art, how great
Thou art!

Then sings my soul, my Savior God, to Thee: how great Thou art, how great
Thou art!

When through the woods and forest glades I wander, and hear the birds sing
sweetly in the trees;

When I look down from lofty mountain grandeur, and hear the brook and
feel the gentle breeze:

(Repeat refrain.)

And when I think that God, His Son not sparing, sent Him to die, I scarce
can take it in;

That on the cross, my burden gladly bearing, He bled and died to take away
my sin:

(Repeat refrain.)

When Christ shall come with shout of acclamation, and take me home, what
joy shall fill my heart!

Then I shall bow in humble adoration, and there proclaim, my God, how
great Thou art!

(Repeat refrain.)

ON YOUR OWN:

Plant a flower seed in a window box or flower pot. As it grows, remind
yourself of the elements of creation that you've just studied, and praise God
for his marvelous work.

NOTES

1. This section is based on *NIVAC: Genesis*, 65–109.
2. Walton, 41–42.
3. Walton, 83.
4. Walton, 30.
5. See Walton, 70–71.
6. This section is based on *NIVAC: Genesis*, 110–120.
7. Walton, 91.
8. This section is based on *NIVAC: Genesis*, 121–145.
9. Walton, 134.
10. Ibid.
11. This section is based on *NIVAC: Genesis*, 146–161.
12. Wenham, Gordon J., *Word Biblical Commentary: Genesis 1–15* (Waco: Tex.: Word, 1987), 37.
13. Walton, 148.
14. *http://en.wikipedia.org/wiki/How_Great_Thou_Art_(Hymn)* (March 22, 2008).

PARADISE LOST

Genesis 2:4 – 4:16

We recently helped some friends move. They didn't have far to go—maybe three miles down the road. But it was a huge organizational endeavor that involved numerous vans, a moving truck, about twenty willing people, and the packing genius and direction of the owners of the house. When all was said and done, everything was in place for a new phase of their lives, but we realized that this was just the beginning. The next step of bringing order out of the chaos of boxes filling every room was not going to be easy, and it would take time before we saw the true blessing of the new house realized. Adam and Eve are in a similar situation beginning in Genesis 2. Following creation, everything is in place for the blessing of God to be realized, but some critical steps need to happen for potential to become reality. We all know the story takes a massive detour, but let's take one step at a time.

SANCTUARY IN THE GARDEN[1]

Read Genesis 2:4 – 25.

1. In the ancient world, it was common for successful kings to have adjacent to their palace a garden featuring fruit and shade trees, watercourses, pools, and paths. It symbolized abundance and peace, the signs of a successful ruler.[2] What features of Eden in Genesis 2 fit this picture? What was Adam's role in the garden?

GOING DEEPER

In 2:15, the role of Adam is identified: God puts him in the garden "to work it and take care of it." . . . [I]t is likely that the tasks given to Adam are of a priestly nature—that is, caring for sacred space. In ancient thinking, caring for sacred space was a way of upholding creation. . . . Maintaining order made one a participant with God in the ongoing task of sustaining the equilibrium God had established in the cosmos.[3]

2. How does this idea from the ancient Near East square up with your picture of Paradise? How does it allow humankind to carry out God's blessing to "be fruitful and increase in number; fill the earth and subdue it" (1:28)?

3. Although the ancient Near East allowed for service to the gods, it was different than we find in Genesis.[4] The traditional gods had needs, especially for food, and gave the jobs they were tired of doing to people. Women were viewed strictly in terms of reproduction, and participated with the king (representing the deity) in fertility rites for the sake of fruitful land. How does Genesis change the dignity for both men and women compared to the traditional Near Eastern views?

4. The Tree of Life has numerous equivalents in other cultures, but the Tree of the Knowledge of Good and Evil is unique to the Bible. The exact meaning of "knowledge of good and evil" is a bit elusive, but it suggests discerning or discriminating wisdom. Without the wisdom that the Tree of the Knowledge of Good and Evil offers, do you think Adam and Eve can be held responsible to obey God's command not to eat from the tree (2:16–17)?

Read Genesis 3:1–7.

5. For the first time, according to the presentation in Genesis, Eve is presented with an option to do something different from what God has said. How does the serpent twist God's words? What convinces Eve to give it a try? How does she rationalize her choice?

6. Since that first act of disobedience, our options for ways of acting out against God have only increased. Just think of the choices available to us today! They're not even necessarily bad desires—even wisdom is something we would put on the "good list," generally speaking. What can we learn from Eve's interaction with the serpent to help us sort out a good choice from a bad one?

LIFE IN A FALLEN WORLD[6]

Read Genesis 3:8 – 24.

7. Besides the death that God declared to be a sure outcome in 2:17, there are immediate consequences to Adam's and Eve's disobedience. How does the evil that has entered the garden affect relationships even prior to God's pronouncement in 3:14 – 19? What evidence do you see of that kind of "bad fruit" continuing today?

8. Is God's blessing revoked with his pronouncement in 3:14 – 19? What specifically is cursed? How are Adam's and Eve's abilities to carry out the blessing affected?

GOING DEEPER

In eating of the fruit, Adam and Eve attempted to gain autonomy and move away from their dependence on God. In his pronouncement, God outlines the trade-offs that have been made. Both Adam and Eve will still be dependent on him to carry out their primary functions and secure the benefits of the blessing. The anguish and anxiety they experience in their functions will constantly exhaust their resources and cast them on God.[7]

9. For the Israelites, the greatest loss from the fall was not focused on their heart condition so much as on their loss of access to the presence of God.[8] Adam is no longer the privileged gardener or sanctuary-keeper for the king of the universe. The struggle for restoration with God characterizes much of the remaining Old Testament. In spite of this, what evidence is there for God's grace in the lives of Adam and Eve?

LIFE OUTSIDE THE GARDEN[9]

Read Genesis 4:1–16.

10. In this first glimpse of life outside of God's sanctuary, what evidence is there of his blessing? What evidence is there that evil lurks nearby? What similarities do you see in the interactions of God and Cain compared to God and Adam/Eve?

GOING DEEPER

Most of the chapters in Genesis either document the advance of sin or the advance of blessing.... In this second narrative of sin, we see the tragic descent from Adam and Eve's sin. Eve was envious of God (3:4–6), Cain was envious of Abel. Eve's actions can be seen in quasi-noble terms (wanting to be like God), while Cain's action has nothing noble about it. Perhaps decline into sin sometimes begins with rationalization or pretensions of nobility. But, as with Cain's bitter violence against his brother, in the end all that is left is seething self-indulgence.[10]

11. Compare the beginning of this session — all the potential in God's protected garden of Eden — with the end — Cain, a restless wanderer, fleeing from the cries of his brother's blood, east of Eden. What strikes you most about this contrast?

12. Evil is a powerful force. It can come from outside of us in the guise of the serpent or his envoys. It can come from within us in the form of desires that we are unable to master. It can come in the form of other people, such as Cain luring his brother to a field to attack him. Life outside the garden of Eden would be overwhelming but for the fact that God still rules supremely over his kingdom — nothing is outside his authority. What aspects of God's character from these first two sessions can give you hope to live in this fallen world?

RESPONDING TO GOD'S WORD

IN YOUR GROUP:

One of the problems we saw in this session was the lack of responsibility for sinful words and actions. Discuss as a group how this has affected you — either as a participant or recipient (or both). No need to go as far afield as the government — keep it personal! (Besides, that would be blame-shifting like Adam and Eve!) How do you see it in children? Adults? How does it affect your relationships? How does it affect your attitude toward God? How are we called to deal with it on this side of the cross? As a group, make a pledge to begin to change your response to sin and keep one another accountable.

ON YOUR OWN:

Take a walk outside. What evidence do you see of the advance of God's blessing carried on generation after generation? What evidence do you see of the advance of sin? Take time to pray, confessing your own participation in the advance of sin and praising God for his blessings and grace over and above all else that happens around us.

NOTES

1. This section is based on *NIVAC: Genesis*, 162–201.
2. Walton, 166–167.
3. Walton, 172, 173, 174.
4. Walton, 186–187.
5. This section is based on *NIVAC: Genesis*, 202–221.
6. This section is based on *NIVAC: Genesis*, 222–258.
7. Walton, 239.
8. Walton, 231.
9. This section is based on *NIVAC: Genesis*, 259–273.
10. Walton, 266–267.

THE NEW WORLD

Genesis 6:9 – 9:29; 11:1 – 9

Family reunions can be mixed blessings. I am privileged to be part of a family that looks forward to getting together to recount the blessings of many generations, even while recognizing hardships of the past. But for some families, the pain of just the thought of gathering together prevents a reunion. In Genesis, the genealogies function a bit like family reunions. They're reminders of blessings—new family members; advances in cities, music, and technology (e.g., 4:17 – 22); and a record of faithfulness (e.g., 5:22). They're also reminders of hardship—death, painful toil, violence (e.g., 4:23 – 24), and wickedness on the increase. I leave it up to you to read the genealogies as an important backdrop (4:17 – 6:8; 10:1 – 32; 11:10 – 32), setting the stage for what takes place in God's unfolding story. The bottom line is not a pretty picture. God concludes in 6:5, "The LORD saw how great the wickedness of the human race had become on the earth, and that every inclination of the thoughts of the human heart was only evil all the time." On that note, we jump into the account of Noah.

THE FLOOD[1]

Read Genesis 6:5 – 8:22.

1. To many people, the story of Noah has been familiar since childhood, so it's important to read the text carefully to see what really is and isn't there. There are many other flood stories from other cultures. They don't prove or disprove the biblical account, but they do allow us to see what other cultures thought was important about the story. The reason for the flood in other ancient Near Eastern accounts was because human overpopulation made too much noise that was bothering the gods. How is the biblical account different from these? What does it reveal about God?

GOING DEEPER

God is the One who operates a system of checks and balances. There is a certain range of variation that is possible in the domain of human behavior. As with the stock market, this range of equilibrium is based on thousands of factors. When a situation needs a "market adjustment," God is responsible for doing that. Just as the chairman of the Federal Reserve oversees the economy and initiates certain adjustments as he deems necessary to sustain a healthy economy, so God oversees the world. The difference is that the chairman of the Federal Reserve does not have absolute control of the economy, whereas God is truly sovereign.[2]

2. Although this is Noah's story, he never speaks a word. In terms of literary structure, scholars identify the focal point of the flood story either in 7:21–24 (the death of all except Noah and his family) or in 8:1 ("but God remembered Noah").[3] In either case, who is the "prime mover" of the story? How do God's actions here parallel the creation account (6:22; 7:5, 9, 16; 8:1, 15–19)?

3. Although the story of Noah is one we display on cribs and tell even our youngest children, it's not one for the faint of heart. The death toll is enormous, and it seems like a rather extreme way to deal with the violence on the earth. Could you argue that God got carried away here? Did he just lose his temper? Was creation a big mistake that he regretted? What evidence in the account points to the contrary?

4. Humanity gets a fresh start after experiencing God's judgment, and Noah begins well by offering a pleasing sacrifice to God (8:20). This theme of living wisely in light of God's judgment continues in the New Testament with the apostle Peter's exhortation to live holy and godly lives in response to an understanding that God does indeed judge (2 Peter 3:11) — God wasn't afraid to judge humanity in Noah's time, and final judgment is yet to come. In what ways do we experience God's judgment in smaller ways today? How can we learn from such experiences and offer pleasing sacrifices to God in response to his work in us?

GOING DEEPER

It is more than just salvation here; God is committed to salvage operations. Noah and his family are saved; the world and human civilization are salvaged. Salvaging involves retrieving that which is valuable from the wreckage.... This is the God who, amidst the carnage of carnality, finds in Augustine a philosophical thinker who lays the foundation for the church's systematic theology. The same God finds and nurtures in each one of us that which transforms our lives from sinful rubble to useful ministry. God is in the business of re-creating, and our lives testify to that grace. We are salvaged from our sin and its condemnation; we are salvaged for ministry and its service to God.[4]

BLESSING RESTORED[5]

Read Genesis 9:1 – 29.

5. If there were hints at parallels between creation and the flood (see question 2), there are many more between Genesis 2 – 3 and Genesis 9. Clearly, the author had these earlier chapters in mind when he told the details of reestablishing God's blessing on earth after the flood. Compare the two accounts. What similarities and differences do you find in:

a. The blessing (1:28; 9:1 – 2)

b. Food provision (1:29 – 30; 9:3)

c. Prohibitions (2:16 – 17; 9:4 – 6)

d. Filling the earth (2:18 – 25; 9:8 – 17)

e. Temptation (3:1 – 7; 9:20 – 23)

f. Curse (3:14 – 19; 9:24 – 27)

6. What is the overall impact of this new beginning in the post-flood world compared to the pre-flood world?

7. God vowed not to destroy life on earth as a whole in the same way again, but that's not to say that individual lives will not be held accountable in judgment. How has the role of carrying out justice shifted in this chapter? How does the accounting for the life of every human being (9:5) fit in with this shift?

8. God reaffirmed after the flood that "every inclination of the human heart is evil from childhood" (8:21). Cain and his descendant Lamech (4:8–12, 23–24) are prime examples! With hearts like that, can we really look out for one another? How well do we do when there are really serious problems—like murder? Capital punishment is one response. How well do we handle situations requiring such drastic attention today?

9. Despite God's instruction, we get caught in cycles of sin that are hard to break. We need something or someone outside ourselves to break the cycle so we can start fresh, as God allowed Noah and his family to start fresh after the flood. How does the account of Noah point ahead to God's provision for a final and ongoing solution to our need for new beginnings?

NEW HEIGHTS OF DISOBEDIENCE[6]

Read Genesis 11:1–9.

Based on an understanding of Near Eastern cultures, the Tower of Babel was most likely in the area of Babylon, where urbanization was beginning to take place. Temple complexes were built, featuring a ziggurat—a high, solid, pyramid-shaped structure that served as steps for the gods to travel between earth and heaven. The god could come down to his temple, receive worship, and bless the people. Gods were conceived of in more humanlike forms at this time, as indicated by statues in the city.[7]

10. How is this concept of the gods at odds with what we have seen in Genesis 1–2, where God formed Adam and placed him in his own garden for his purposes?

11. You might be inclined to criticize the people who built the Tower of Babel. How could anyone think that a god of their own creation could do anything for them? But think about our own expectations of God. In what ways do we put him in a box and expect him to serve our needs?

GOING DEEPER

By nature we are all pagans caught in the Babel syndrome. When we think we can manipulate God by praying in Jesus' name to achieve selfish purposes, our paganism is showing. When we "claim promises" as a means of making God do what we want him to do, our paganism is showing. When we come to think we are indispensable to God because of the money we donate, the talents we have, the ministries we engage in, or the worship we offer, our paganism is showing. When we treat God as a child to be cajoled or a tyrant to be appeased, the Babel syndrome is surging in our veins.[8]

12. Given the perversion of the people's understanding of God represented by the Tower of Babel, how would confusing their language and scattering them help accomplish God's purposes? How does this set the scene for the rest of Genesis?

RESPONDING TO GOD'S WORD

IN YOUR GROUP:

Find a recent newspaper article that concerns the death penalty. Summarize the article and then discuss the following: How is the respect for human life addressed? What issues make it a hot topic in our society? How does the Bible address both sides of the issue? How can Christians be involved in this issue in a godly way?

ON YOUR OWN:

When you shower this week, think about the flood and how it washed away the unrighteousness in the world. Pray that you would begin the day fresh with the sweet aroma of God's forgiveness, and think about how you can be a living sacrifice for the new day.

NOTES

1. This section is based on *NIVAC: Genesis*, 304–338.
2. Walton, 334.
3. Walton, 316.
4. Walton, 338.
5. This section is based on *NIVAC: Genesis*, 339–363.
6. This section is based on *NIVAC: Genesis*, 364–387.
7. Walton, 372–374.
8. Walton, 383.

ABRAHAM'S NEW CALLING

Genesis 11:27 – 14:24

Growing up is an interesting process to watch. Little ones start out with everything being done for them, but wise parents encourage their children from an early age to reach out and try new things. Of course there are the physical steps: learning to crawl, then walk, then develop further skills as children grow older. Equally interesting is the development of thought processes, social skills, and emotional maturity. In each case, there's a balance between learning how to become more independent while maintaining an appropriate degree of dependence and relationship with parents or guardians as an individual grows up. There are some interesting parallels in the beginning chapters of Genesis—from Adam and Eve, utterly dependent on God, learning simple rules of obedience, moving on to Abram, who grows in maturity as God extends his boundaries and experiences, changing but growing in his relationship to God and his understanding of God's promises to him.

BLESSING REDEFINED[1]

Read Genesis 11:27 – 12:20.

1. The covenant, or agreement, that God made with Noah (9:17) was about a promise that he made to all people. From Noah and his sons, many nations were established (10:1–32). But as we saw in the last session, God had to take action so people wouldn't spread the wrong kinds of ideas too extensively (i.e., the Tower of Babel, 11:1–9). How does the call of Abram (12:2–3) show a shift in how God's blessing on people is carried out?

GOING DEEPER

[T]he nature of the blessing on the nations is that God has revealed himself through Abram's family. The law was given through them; the prophets were from among their number; Scripture was written by them; and their history became a public record of God's attributes in action. Then to climax it all, his own Son came through them and revealed the Father and the kingdom through his life and a plan of salvation for the world through his death. In Abram all the nations of the earth were blessed as they were shown what God was like and as the means were provided for them to become justified, reconciled to God, and forgiven of their sins.[2]

2. It's important to follow the blessing theme that's been threading through Genesis so far—basically how people will produce both food and offspring. Put yourself in Abram's sandals for a minute. What are the risks he faces by following God's call to leave his country, his people, and his father's household? How do God's promises go above and beyond what he asks Abram to give up?

3. Abram picks up his tent and heads to Canaan. He arrives with his barren wife in an occupied land facing famine and the Lord tells him, "To your offspring I will give this land" (12:7). The blessing, though essentially the same, has gotten more complicated since God put Adam and Eve in the garden. Compare God's provision of food and offspring in the garden (2:16, 22), after the fall (4:1−2), and now (12:7, 10). How have things changed? Would you say things are improving for Abram? Why or why not?

4. When we read about Abram's time in Egypt (12:10–20), we generally get caught up in Abram's deception, when he tells Pharaoh that Sarai is his sister, not his wife. But the author of Genesis actually makes no comment on whether that was good or bad, or how it was understood in those days. Instead of focusing on questions *we* have about this incident, think about it in terms of God's promised blessing. How does this incident put God's blessing on Abram at further risk?

5. How does God work through the situation in Egypt to put the blessing of Abram's family back on track? What does this tell you about God?

GOING DEEPER

[C]hapter 12 sets the tone for the next ten chapters as advance and jeopardy [of the covenant] are intertwined. God will demonstrate again and again his ability to overcome obstacles and resolve jeopardy as he fulfills promises and provides what is necessary for the covenant to move forward.

In this way we can again see that the author's purpose is focused on God, not on using Abram for a role model.... The Bible is not trying to teach us how to act or how not to act by Abram's example. The events are presented in a straightforward manner, without commitment, to demonstrate how God overcame the obstacle that seemed ready to dismantle the covenant piece by piece.[3]

LAND OF PROMISE[4]

Read Genesis 13:1 – 18.

6. At last there are hints that things are progressing for Abram. He's in the Promised Land and doing quite well there. What evidence do you see in Genesis 13 that God is continuing to work through human decision-making to advance the promise of blessing for Abram? What foreshadowing is there that Lot's decision won't incur the same sort of favor?

7. We as readers are given the information that Sodom was wicked (13:13). But is there anything inherently right or wrong in the decision-making of Abram and Lot regarding their choice of territory? Explain. How does this compare to decisions you've had to make in your life that are potentially life-changing?

8. Lot accompanied Abram to the Promised Land, and both were blessed with extensive possessions. Nothing wrong with that — but Lot was a potential obstacle to God's blessing of Abram because of limited resources. As you think about your own life, is there anything (not necessarily sinful) that could potentially be an obstacle to understanding God's work in your life in a deeper way? Can you see any way those circumstances might change in the future?

FIRST TASTE OF CONQUEST[5]

Read Genesis 14:1–24.

Melchizedek is one of the most mysterious figures in Scripture, partially because of the Jewish thought and traditions that developed beyond what is actually in the biblical text. The references to him in the book of Hebrews (Heb. 5:10; 6:20; 7:1, 2, 10, 11, 15, 17) come partially out of that tradition. For the sake of Genesis, however, it is more helpful to think about the context that is presented here — namely that he appears to be a regional king who was predominant over other kings in the area, which would not have been unusual at that time.[6]

9. Even though it's hard to pin down exactly who all the kings are in Genesis 14 and where they're from, we can tell there was conflict over Canaan. Why does Abram get involved in the fray? What does it tell you about his resources? How does he fare?

10. Keep in mind that Abram was the new man on the block here. He came to Canaan because God gave him the land, but the people living there probably didn't know that nor would they have recognized God's authority to give it to him. How would Abram's defeat of the kings change his status among the regional kings according to typical "might wins the day" sort of rules? How could this help the advance of his "great nation" status according to the covenant? Do you think this was Abram's intention? Why or why not?

11. The meal Abram and Melchizedek share (14:18) typically indicates a peaceful agreement.[7] The fact that Abram gives Melchizedek an offering (14:20) points to his willingness to allow Melchizedek to continue as the predominant king in the area, despite Abram's victory. The king of Sodom's statement (14:21) indicates that Abram has rights to all the booty from the skirmish. What do Abram's interactions with Melchizedek and the king of Sodom reveal about Abram's mind-set? How does it compare to Adam and Eve's mind-set regarding advancement?

GOING DEEPER

Certainly there are times when God wants us to step out in faith rather than sit around and wait for him to do something. But there are times when submitting is better than seizing as we seek to achieve our potential in his service and plan. Abram gave up a chance for the land, eventually to gain the land. David gave up a chance for the crown, eventually to gain the crown. Christ gave up a chance for the kingdoms, eventually to gain the kingdom. When preparing ourselves for our role in God's plan or to receive God's blessing, it is often counterproductive to take the easy way to the goal. It can be disastrous to simply seize what lies before us.[8]

12. What do you do when two people give you advice, but that advice is completely at odds? "*Carpe diem!* Seize the day!" versus "Let's wait and see" can both be appropriate responses in given situations. How do you discern what's the right thing to do? How does Abram's situation shed light on such a dilemma?

RESPONDING TO GOD'S WORD

IN YOUR GROUP:

Think about key decisions in your life that either changed or confirmed a direction you were headed. As you look back, were they self-directed or God-directed decisions? Share with the group how you can see God working through one of those key decisions as you look back now.

ON YOUR OWN:

Read the following quote by C. S. Lewis from *Screwtape Letters* about the power of "nothing":

Nothing is very strong: strong enough to steal away a man's best years, not in sweet sins but in a dreary flickering of the mind over it knows not what and knows not why, in the gratification of curiosities so feeble that the man is only half aware of them, in drumming of fingers and kicking of heels, in whistling tunes that he does not like, or in the long, dim labyrinth of reveries that have not even lust or ambition to give them a relish, but which, once chance association has started them, man is too weak and feeble and fuddled to shake off.[9]

Think about ways in which you are subject to the power of "nothing." Take note of times you catch yourself doing this sort of thing during the week. Pray that you would be subject to the King of Creation's plans for you instead of being subject to "nothing."

NOTES

1. This section is based on *NIVAC: Genesis*, 388–410.
2. Walton, 402.
3. Walton, 398.
4. This section is based on *NIVAC: Genesis*, 411–415, 424–426, 432–434.
5. This section is based on *NIVAC: Genesis*, 416–419, 426–427, 434–436.
6. Walton, 418–419, 426–427.
7. Walton, 419.
8. Walton, 434–435.
9. Quoted in Walton, 434.

SESSION 5

AN HEIR IN
THE MAKING

Genesis 15:1 – 18:15

Infertility is an issue that cuts deeply to the heart. Early in my marriage, when I was working in South Asia with an agrarian-based culture, one of the first questions I was asked was whether I was married and how many children I had. They wondered what was wrong with me when I replied that I didn't have children yet. Even with all the scientific advancements we've made, and the culturally acceptable alternatives to bearing your own children, that question still affects people deeply — the gift of life is still something we regard as quite miraculous. On the other extreme, fertility becomes an issue when pregnancy is unwanted, inconvenient, or the incubating infant is not quite to our liking, creating volatile issues that divide people. In Abram's time, a woman's fertility was almost equivalent with her worth — so much depended on producing an heir. Abram and Sarai were painfully aware of this while they went on day after day, year after year, building a life in Canaan.

BELIEVING GOD[1]

Read Genesis 15:1 – 21.

1. Just as we have various ways of dealing with infertility, so did Abram's culture. A male servant could be named an heir, or a child could be "incubated" by a female servant.[2] But obviously these were not ideal—merely secondary solutions to a problem. In a time of great uncertainty for Abram, how does the Lord reassure him (15:1, 4–5, 7)? How does Abram respond (15:6, 8)? New Testament writers refer to Abraham (Abram's later name) as a model of faith (Rom. 3:28–4:3, 18–24; Gal. 3:1–9). Why?

2. When Adam needed help in the garden, God took it upon himself to deal with the solution (2:18–25). How is God's response to Abram similar? How is it different?

3. God's promise to Abram was very specific to his situation—not a general promise that we can claim for our own circumstances. However, God does make certain claims for all believers. Are there times when you have had to take God at his word without knowing the details? How does that affect your relationship with him? What enables you or prohibits you from trusting him?

SARAH CONCEIVES A PLAN[3]

Read Genesis 16:1 – 16.

After ten years of waiting for an heir in Canaan, and with no further instructions from God, Sarai takes steps to clear the obstacle of her own infertility in order to fulfill God's plan for Abram. In the ancient world, using a servant as a surrogate child-bearer was not only acceptable, at times it was dictated.[4]

4. Compare the reasoning of Sarai and Abram in 16:1 – 4 with the reasoning of Eve and Adam in 3:6 – 7. How are they similar? How are they different? How does the resulting "fruit" of the incidents compare in 3:8 – 13, 15; and 16:4 – 6, 12? What conclusions can you draw from your comparisons?

5. In 15:1 the Lord had told Abram in a vision, "Do not be afraid, Abram. I am your shield, your very great reward." If you were to evaluate the events of Genesis 16, who seems to be the recipient of the blessing given to Abram? Explain. How does this reconcile with the promise first given to Abram in 12:2 – 3? What does it reveal about God's character?

6. God may have been a source of comfort to Hagar, but Sarai's situation hasn't greatly improved. Ishmael, though her surrogate son, is a constant reminder of her own inability to bear children. Personal gods in that time period were thought of like good-luck charms, but impossible to predict. Was God just bringing Sarai bad luck? How would you explain the difference between a personal, man-made god and the true God to Sarai? How would you explain years of "bad luck" in a Christian's life today?

THE SIGN OF THE COVENANT[5]

Read Genesis 17:1–27.

7. Most Christians are so familiar with Isaac being part of the covenant promise that Ishmael seems like a blip in the course of history. Not so in other cultures—in fact, Muslims still consider Ishmael the chosen son of God. Put yourselves in Abram's sandals again for a moment. Keep in mind the degree (or lack) of detail that God gave Abram in Genesis 15. According to the information we have, when does God inform Abram that Ishmael is not actually the heir he was talking about? For how many years is he mistaken (17:24)? How might relationships in Abram's family be affected by their misperceptions during that time? How might their (mis)understanding impact the covenant?

8. God spells out the covenant with Abraham much more specifically in Genesis 17. Compare 12:2–3 and 15:4–21 with 17:1–22. What new elements does God let Abraham in on?

9. Hebrew names have much more significance culturally than American names typically do. Yet we all recognize the power of identity in a name. What do name changes mean in your own culture? What do you think it meant to Abram ("exalted father") for God to change his name to Abraham ("father of many")?

GOING DEEPER

God does not give each of us new names when we enter into relationship with him, nor do we adopt new names when baptized. Nevertheless, the concept that we are joyfully submitting to a new master is no less significant and deserves visible recognition. In medieval times soldiers were sworn to allegiance by being dubbed as knights. Their fealty thereafter belonged to that lord. It is perhaps our loss that we no longer display our allegiance so visibly.... Though we no longer adopt Christian names, it is essential that we find our identity in Christ, pledge our allegiance to Christ, and count Christ as the benefactor of all blessings. This is what it means to be named in Christ; it is the same concept as is represented in Abraham's receiving a new name.[6]

10. Circumcision was not a brand new idea during this time—it was used widely as a rite of puberty or marriage throughout the ancient Near East—but this is the first time the idea is adopted as a theological statement.[7] What statement does it make in regard to an outward sign of the covenant with God? What does Abraham's response indicate about his attitude toward God at this time?

GOD REVEALS HIS PLAN TO SARAH[8]

Read Genesis 18:1–15.

11. In one sense, nothing new is revealed in these verses besides Abraham's generosity to strangers—God had already told Abraham in the last chapter that Isaac would be born to Sarah within a year. But the interaction with Sarah seems pretty significant. How does Sarah react to the news that at last she will have a son? How does her interaction with the Lord's messenger demonstrate another advance for the covenant?

12. Consider how gradually and personally God revealed elements of the covenant to Abraham and Sarah. Although we have much more information available to us than they did (because we have God's completed revelation in the Bible, including God coming in the flesh as Jesus), our understanding of him often comes gradually as well, including misunderstandings and doubts such as Abraham and Sarah experienced. How has your own experience of God grown over the years? Has your identity been influenced by your understanding of who God is? Explain.

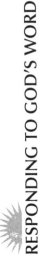

RESPONDING TO GOD'S WORD

IN YOUR GROUP:

Take about five minutes either to go outside or look around the room that you're meeting in. Find an object that can represent your identity in some way. For example, a withered leaf might say something about your emotional state. A throw pillow might represent how flexible you are. After you've all found something, take turns sharing with the group why you picked what you did and what it says about you.

ON YOUR OWN:

Many psalms are laments, crying out to God when things are tough. They can serve as a template for how to express your frustrations and longings, such as Sarah must have felt over her many long years of infertility. Most (but not all) laments end by turning to God and realizing his faithfulness. Begin with Psalm 13. Think about Sarah's situation as well as any difficulties of your own. Skim through other psalms during the week and take note of laments that can help you cry out to God when you need to.

NOTES

1. This section is based on *NIVAC: Genesis*, 420–423, 428–432, 436–441.
2. Walton, 454.
3. This section is based on *NIVAC: Genesis*, 442–449, 454–455, 469–470.
4. Walton, 445–446.
5. This section is based on *NIVAC: Genesis*, 449–451, 455–461, 467–469.
6. Walton, 468.
7. Walton, 450–451.
8. This section is based on *NIVAC: Genesis*, 452–454, 462–466, 470–471.

ADVANCES FOR
THE COVENANT

Genesis 18:16–21:34

D o you ever wonder if just one person can really make a difference? When you think in terms of voting and public opinion, it sometimes seems so futile — one voice so easily gets lost in the noise of the crowd. But then I hear of people who have single-mindedly devoted their lives to something they believe in, and it's refreshing to realize what a huge impact a person can have. A much-loved elementary school principal in our area retired a few years ago. When I spoke to some of the parents bemoaning the loss, they consistently spoke of his character and the environment of encouragement, hard work, and respect he fostered through his work at the school — impacting more people than he'll ever know. One person does make a difference, and God put that principle to work in choosing Abraham to be a blessing to the nations.

PLEADING FOR THE RIGHTEOUS[1]

Read Genesis 18:16–33.

1. We often come to this passage thinking that Abraham is bargaining with God to try to save Lot and his family, as he saved Lot before in Genesis 14. However, the Lord's discussion of the covenant (18:17–19) could imply a bigger purpose to Abraham's questions.[2] The Lord reemphasizes that all nations will be blessed through Abraham (18:18). What is the source of blessing available to Abraham to potentially bless the nations around him? If Sodom and Gomorrah are destroyed, what opportunity will Abraham have for blessing them?

2. In 18:23, Abraham poses a philosophical question to God: "Will you sweep away the righteous with the wicked?" He strongly appeals to God's sense of justice not to do such a thing (18:24–25). Think through the alternative. How are the righteous and the wicked treated if God spares the city? What other alternative could Abraham be arguing for in light of his covenant responsibilities to the nations?

If there were fifty righteous, would God spare the city for a time to see if that righteous minority could have an impact in the city and turn it around? What opportunity will be given for the minority to bring about change? How small can the minority be and still be allowed to have an impact? This is an important issue for Abraham to explore because his family is to be that righteous minority among the nations, with Sodom standing as a representative microcosm.[3]

3. What is your own experience of the minority having an impact on society? Are there lessons from history that bear on the question? What implications are there for Christians being light in the world?

SODOM AND GOMORRAH DESTROYED[4]

Read Genesis 19:1–29.

4. What evidence is there that Lot is trying to have a positive impact on the city of Sodom? How effective is he?

5. In the destruction of Sodom and Gomorrah, has the Judge of all the earth done right (18:25)? What evidence do you see of God's grace and mercy in the midst of it all?

GOING DEEPER

The sin of the Sodomites is self-evident and multileveled, blatant and unambiguous. The standard is not the later Mosaic law but civilized behavior regulated by laws in every city and country. There is nothing subtle or secretive about their behavior. No inhibitions interfere with their threats of violence or demands to indulge their lust. The last thing anyone in the reading audience would be expected to do would be to come to the defense of Sodom or try to make excuses for their behavior.[5]

6. Jesus compares the coming of the kingdom of God, analogous to the final judgment, with the destruction of Sodom. It will come suddenly — in the midst of living out life, not when we have a sense of being "finished" (Luke 17:27 – 30). There won't be any opportunity to go back and retrieve what we consider precious (17:31 – 32). What does this tell you about Lot's wife and her demise? Is there a warning in this for you? Explain.

MAKING WAY FOR THE COVENANT[6]

Read Genesis 19:30–38.

7. Incest was already viewed negatively by the ancient world at this time, and would have been reprehensible to the original audience.[7] It's likely that this passage is not here intended as a commentary on incest, but rather to show the origins of the Moabites and Ammonites, who lived directly east of the Promised Land.[8] What does their origin tell you about their relationship to the covenant? What would this communicate to the later generations of Abraham as they faced these nations on their way into the Promised Land?

Read Genesis 20:1–18 and 21:22–34.

8. This is the second incident where we've read that Abraham passed Sarah off as his sister, although 20:13 suggests he did it numerous times. As we've said before, we don't really know how this was culturally viewed. But both incidents put the covenant promises in greater jeopardy. How would that be the case in this incident? What actions does God take to protect the covenant promises?

9. Abraham justifies his actions by reasoning that there was "no fear of God in this place" (20:11). Would you agree with Abraham? Why or why not? What does Abimelech learn of God in his interactions with Abraham? What does Abraham learn of God in his interactions with Abimelech?

GOING DEEPER

Gradually Abraham is establishing roots in the land—digging wells and planting trees. Additionally, as relationships are established with the peoples in the land, the blessing is taking root. Finally, the relationship with God is taking root as land and family become established.[9]

FULFILLED PROMISES[10]

Read Genesis 21:1–21 and 25:12–18.

10. After all the buildup about an heir, the birth of Isaac seems to slip by almost too quickly, but it is cause for great joy. Think about Sarah before and after Isaac's birth. How will Isaac's name ("laughter") be a reminder of God's promises? How do you see the covenant advancing in these passages?

11. In some ways, sending off Hagar and Ishmael seems like a darker side to the covenant, and indeed it was hard on Abraham (21:11). However, God's hand is seen clearly in their lives as well. How does the author show God's fulfillment of promises to Hagar and Abraham (compare 25:12–18 to 16:7–16 and 17:20)?

12. Sometimes we tend to romanticize the virtues of the Bible characters when we're not familiar with the details of the text. In reality, they struggle with the same kind of day-to-day decisions that we do in living out a life of faith. Some things they do make sense, some don't. They're not meant to be models of virtue. And yet, God works through them. How can this be an encouragement to you in trying to have an impact on the world as a Christian?

RESPONDING TO GOD'S WORD

IN YOUR GROUP:

Consider the following quote by C. S. Lewis:[11]

If you think of this world as a place intended simply for our happiness, you find it quite intolerable: think of it as a place of training or correction and it's not so bad.

How does this thought compare to the stories of the people we've seen in Genesis? How about with your own life? How does it reflect the advance of the covenant?

ON YOUR OWN:

Make a list of your strengths. Talk to a couple other people who know you well and see if they would agree with you. How has God used your strengths to have an impact on others? How could they be used more effectively to build his kingdom?

NOTES

1. This section is based on *NIVAC: Genesis*, 472–476, 482–487.
2. Walton, 482–483.
3. Ibid.
4. This section is based on *NIVAC: Genesis*, 476–480, 487–490.
5. Walton, 476–477.
6. This section is based on *NIVAC: Genesis*, 480–481, 484–485, 491–500.
7. Walton, 481.
8. Walton, 484.
9. Walton, 502.
10. This section is based on *NIVAC: Genesis*, 496–498, 500–506, 533.
11. C. S. Lewis, *God in the Dock: Essays on Theology and Ethics* (The Trustees of the Estate of C. S. Lewis, 1970), 52.

A TEST
OF LOVE

Genesis 22:1–19; 23:1–20; 25:1–11

Wᵉ've all taken tests. Some are more memorable than others. Have you ever thought about how the test also measures the person giving it, not just the person taking it? How about the road test for your driver's license — it always seems like the person sitting next to you exudes power over your life as he or she commands you to perform certain maneuvers. I'll never forget one final exam I took that was only a couple of questions, but incredibly creative in applying all I had studied — I kept thinking about it for days afterward, and grew in my respect for the teacher who challenged us to use the material that way. Then there was a high school teacher who designed his tests so that no one was likely to finish, causing some to fail for the first time in their lives, supposedly because that had been done to him in his past. What does that say about the test giver? In this session we will look at the testing of Abraham, which also seemed doomed to failure on many levels, yet what we learn about the test giver expands our understanding of God tremendously — both in what he expects of us and how he provides above and beyond our imagination.

THREE LONG DAYS¹

Read Genesis 22:1–12.

1. After all the progress that's been made toward advancing the covenant and settling the lives of Abraham and Sarah, this test comes as quite a shocker! How is this obstacle to the covenant different from others we've encountered so far (such as leaving the Promised Land, pretending Sarah is Abraham's sister, using Hagar as a surrogate mother)? Why do you suppose God asked Abraham to do such a thing?

2. The author doesn't give us any insight into Abraham's feelings, although they're not hard to imagine. From what we've learned of Abraham so far (e.g., 21:11; 22:2), what would make it hard to sacrifice Isaac? How would his three-day journey make it even harder?

GOING DEEPER

Abraham's compliant acquiescence, as much as it reflects the power of his faith, also suggests that human sacrifice is familiar to his conceptual worldview. However saddened he may have been, he is not dumbfounded by the macabre or peculiar nature of Yahweh's demand. It was culturally logical, despite being emotionally harsh, and only baffling in light of the covenant promises.[2]

3. When God told Abraham to leave his country, his people, and his father's household, he also gave Abraham the promise of a new land, his own family, and a relationship with God himself who would provide blessings reaching far into the future (12:1–3). How is the command to sacrifice Isaac different? How does it raise the bar on a test of Abraham's faith?

GOING DEEPER

Has Abraham's faith been motivated by personal gain or simply by his love for God? Up until this point one does not know which is true. Maybe Abraham himself does not know for sure. This test allows the patriarch to demonstrate to himself, to Isaac, to the world, but most of all to God that his faith is not driven by what he will receive out of it but by his commitment to God. God and God alone motivates his faith — he is willing to give up all he stands to gain, all he loves, all he hopes for.[3]

4. In a day when the prosperity gospel is often not far below the surface (believing in God because of the improved life he promises), we tend to put God to the test for his promises to us rather than submitting to God's testing our faith. Does your faith have "conditions" on it? What do you expect out of God beyond the joy of knowing him? Be honest with yourself!

5. Depending on what we hold dearest, God tests us in different ways. For Abraham, it was his willingness to sacrifice Isaac. For the rich young ruler in Luke 18:18–23, it was his possessions. The things (or people) that we love are not necessarily bad things, but they can still get in the way of our love to God. Suppose God came to you and asked you to give up the thing that is most important to you. What do you think it would it be? Could you do it? Explain.

 GOING DEEPER

> Would we give God a chance if there were nothing in it for us? Would we give God our lives if he gave nothing back but himself? Would our lives have a place for God if we were "living for today"? It should be our aspiration to respond to those questions with a resounding "yes!" That is what Abraham did when he built his altar on Mount Moriah and bound his son. God asks no less of us than to be our all in all.[4]

6. The author emphasizes the importance of Isaac in Abraham's life with his repetitive language in 22:2, 12, and 16—Isaac is his *son*, his *only son*, the *son whom he loves*. Because Abraham was still willing to sacrifice Isaac, God knew Abraham feared him (22:12). How can this incident point us to greater knowledge of God's love for us, looking at the language of Matthew 3:16–17; 17:5; John 3:16; and 1 John 4:9–10?

THE LORD'S PROVISION[5]

Read Genesis 22:13–19.

Some of the previous questions are admittedly tough—do I really love God so much that I'd be willing to give up everything else? What if I've got a little faith, but I know I'm not as committed as I should be? What if I'm not as good a Christian as the person sitting next to me? The good news of the gospel is NOT that if I tense up my faith-muscles harder, screw up my courage, and try really, really hard I'll be a little more like Abraham. The good news of the gospel is that Abraham looked up and there in a thicket he saw a ram caught by its horns (22:13). What a picture of grace—the Lord will provide!

7. In the unfolding story of the covenant, what did Abraham learn from the place he called "The Lord Will Provide"? What did it mean to the original audience (the wandering Israelites) that "The Lord Will Provide"? What does it mean to you?

8. By naming the place where God prevented the sacrifice of Isaac "The Lord Will Provide," Abraham acknowledges that God takes care of even the details of those he loves. In 21:33 when Abraham was in the land of the Philistines, he called on the Lord *El Olam*, "The Eternal God," showing how God is responsible for the grand scheme of things. In the ancient Near East, there would have been many different gods fulfilling different roles that are all fulfilled by The Eternal God.[6] How do these names for God complement each other? How could it transform the ancients' understanding of God?

9. In 22:16 God swears by himself, then states his covenant promises for a fourth time. How does this strengthen his covenant promise? Why is swearing by himself more effective at this point than it would have been when he first spoke to Abraham?

10. What details are added to the covenant promises in 22:17 – 18 compared to those in 12:2 – 3; 15:13 – 21; and 17:2 – 22? What significance would they have to the original Israelites hearing it?

THE DEATHS OF SARAH AND ABRAHAM[7]

Read Genesis 23:1 – 20 and 25:1 – 11.

11. The final chapters concerning Abraham and Sarah serve to tie up loose ends, but they focus particularly on the advance of the covenant, which is appropriate considering how important it's been in their lives. What specific elements pave the way for the blessing to continue in future generations?

12. Often when we think of a "blessed" life, we think of smooth sailing and happiness. Considering the various ups and downs that Abraham and Sarah faced during their lives, would you call their lives "blessed"? Do we need to redefine the term? Explain.

[C]onfusing "ideal" with "normal" is a mistake many make regarding their expectations in life. Somehow we have come to the conclusion that a normal life is one that glides along above the fray with nothing to interfere with health, happiness, and prosperity. We may even consider such things are "rights," owed to us by society, the constitution, or God. Then when something disrupts that calm stability, we begin to wonder why God has done this to us. We need to adjust our expectations and come to a new definition of "normal."[8]

RESPONDING TO GOD'S WORD

IN YOUR GROUP:

Some people consider roller coasters frightening; others think they're exhilarating. How about the people in your group? John Walton attributes the sensation to a sense of control — the anxiety related to your trust in whether the cars will stay on the tracks or not. By analogy, the level of anxiety in your life can be connected to your sense of control.

The distance between a response of fear and one of exhilaration is the belief we have that the situation truly is under control, even if it is not our control.... We may feel that we are free-falling through life, but we are held by God, who is in absolute control. It may not quite be exhilaration that we feel when life takes a dive, but having faith that the situation is never out of God's control and that we are still on the tracks can calm our fears.[9]

Would you agree or disagree? How does your anxiety level relate to your sense of God's control in your life?

ON YOUR OWN:

Some people focus their faith on doing what pleases God. Others would focus on rejoicing in his provision, as in seeing the ram caught in the thicket. How would you characterize your own attitude? Do you focus on your own sacrifices or on God's grace in your life? How does it affect your view of God?

NOTES

1. This section is based on *NIVAC: Genesis*, 507–510, 512–520.
2. Walton, 510.
3. Walton, 515.
4. Walton, 520.
5. This section is based on *NIVAC: Genesis*, 511–512, 520–521.
6. Walton, 516.
7. This section is based on *NIVAC: Genesis*, 522–529, 532–535.
8. Walton, 517.
9. Walton, 517–518.

TWISTS AND TURNS IN THE COVENANT

Genesis 24; 25:19 – 28:9

I love a good spy movie. There are so many unpredictable elements that are cleverly knit together, usually starring a debonair mastermind who can work all kinds of nifty gadgets to his advantage, smoothly bringing everything to a stunning conclusion that leaves your heart racing. Then there are comedies or spoofs where absolutely everything goes wrong, but somehow everything works out in the end for the bungling detective anyway. Real life probably falls somewhere in the middle, weighted toward the comedy, although to the people involved it might not seem so comic, nor does it always end happily. Personalities get involved that make it much harder to laugh at some of our circumstances. As the covenant moves ahead in the next couple of generations, there is no lack of drama. The amazing thing is that God knits it altogether for his purposes.

A SUITABLE WIFE FOR ISAAC[1]

Read Genesis 24.

1. Abraham seems to be doing quite well in his old age, but the covenant is a promise that pertains to future generations. What indications are there in the beginning of Genesis 24 that the covenant is advancing? What potential risks are there to the covenant? How does Abraham deal with them?

2. What evidence do you see of growth in Abraham's faith and obedience compared to earlier chapters in his life? How does his understanding of God spread to others?

3. Abraham's servant uses an oracle,[2] that is a test, to determine God's will for choosing Isaac's wife (24:14). What are the risks of using such a technique? What does it tell you about the servant's faith? What does it tell you about God?

GOING DEEPER

A camel that has gone a few days without water can drink as much as twenty-five gallons. Ancient jars used for drawing water usually held no more than three gallons. In other words, this offer involves perhaps from eighty to a hundred drawings from the well. Such an unbelievable proposal would indicate that God is working to override human nature in specified ways. In choosing this mechanism, the servant is not attempting to identify certain qualities in the girl. He intentionally selects an extreme alternative that is not just unlikely but totally outside the realm of possibility in order for there to be no doubt that God is controlling the situation. If deity provides the answer, he can alter normal behavior and override natural instinct in order to communicate his answer.[3]

4. Do you look for "signs" to determine God's will? How reliable are your tests? What other means do we have to determine God's will?

Instead of asking for miraculous signs, we should ask God to help us to be motivated only by what pleases and honors him. We should ask him to help us think clearly about the decision and to direct our thinking. If we faithfully do our part, it is then his job to guide us to the right decision. He can do this through abnormal circumstances that carry his unmistakable mark, but more frequently he will do it through closed and open doors, through our own thinking process, and through his Spirit working within us. Asking for signs may indicate that we do not trust God enough to allow him to work in our minds and hearts to give us godly discernment.[4]

GOING DEEPER

IN HIS FATHER'S FOOTSTEPS[5]

Read Genesis 25:19–26:35.

5. In some ways, the account of Isaac seems like a compressed form of Abraham's story. What incidents remind you of events in Abraham's life? By choosing these events to tell, what impression does the author convey about Isaac's life?

6. Isaac's story of blessing is sandwiched between hints of brewing conflict. What do you see in this section that might suggest that the third generation will not be as straightforward as the second generation?

7. The birthright incident (25:27–34) introduces the differences and conflict that set in between Esau and Jacob. Who is at fault? What do you learn about Esau's and Jacob's characters?

BLESSING FOR WHOM?[6]

Read Genesis 27:1–28:9.

GOING DEEPER

Isaac is planning to give the patriarchal blessing, which must be distinguished from the material inheritance (birthright) discussed at the end of Genesis 25. The blessing has nothing to do with material goods or birth order. It is also important to distinguish the patriarchal blessing from the covenant blessing, though there may be areas of overlap. The covenant blessing is passed on to Jacob by Isaac in 28:3–4, but more important, is confirmed by God in subsequent settings.[7]

8. God's revelation teaches us about who God is. But it also reveals a lot about human nature. God told Cain, "If you do what is right, will you not be accepted? But if you do not do what is right, sin is crouching at your door; it desires to have you, but you must rule over it" (4:7). What better place than a family to see what happens when people rub shoulders with one another? Think about the family dynamics in this chapter. What areas of weakness or temptation do you see in each family member?

9. How might each family member be contributing toward putting the covenant in jeopardy? Think in particular about how this section contrasts with the careful steps that were taken with Isaac in the second generation of the covenant.

10. Take a couple of minutes to think about Rebekah's and Jacob's plot to trick Isaac. Genesis 27:1 rules out sight as a means Isaac has of confirming the identity of his son, but he makes use of his four other senses: touch, hearing, taste, and smell. How effective were each of the tests? What is the likelihood that Jacob's deception would work (including the timing of it all)?

11. In 28:1–9 the covenant promises seem to take another turn. What elements suggest the advancement of the covenant? What risks remain? What does this say about God's ability to overcome obstacles?

12. God told Cain to master his desires so that he wouldn't give in to temptation and sin (4:7). He told Abraham to walk before him and be blameless (17:1). God's continued blessing is conditional on obedience (26:4–5). Yet he takes sinful human nature into account and uses it to accomplish his purposes of advancing the covenant and making his ways known to all nations through Abraham's family. Is this inconsistent? How can you explain the responsibility we have for our actions and God's ability to make good of circumstances in spite of our actions?

RESPONDING TO GOD'S WORD

IN YOUR GROUP:

Personalities add an interesting dimension to any group interaction, whether in a family, small group, church, or any other setting. Is there a personality type that is "more Christian"? Discuss among yourselves the dynamics that personality adds in groups you've been in and the temptations that might go along with them—whether there is a mix of personalities or all one "type."

ON YOUR OWN:

Think about your own personality. How did God design you? How can God use your personality to build his kingdom? What weaknesses or blind spots do you need to be aware of as you interact with others?

NOTES

1. This section is based on *NIVAC: Genesis*, 529–532, 534–541.
2. "In an oracle a yes/no question is posed to deity and a mechanism of some binary nature is given so that deity can provide an answer (the oracle)" (Walton, 530). In popular language we might say the servant is putting a "fleece" before the Lord. See Judges 6:36–40 for the origin of this term.
3. Walton, 530.
4. Walton, 540–541.
5. This section is based on *NIVAC: Genesis*, 542–553, 556–561.
6. This section is based on *NIVAC: Genesis*, 554–556, 562–570.
7. Walton, 554.

A JOURNEY OF FAITH

Genesis 28:10–33:20

When I look back over my own life, it's helpful to think of it as a journey. I can see movement in a certain direction, with various side trips, detours, and stops that are memorable. There have been certain junctions that have been particularly significant—major decisions that led in a certain direction and had further significance down the road. There have been times that I want to put a marker in the road, or include a snapshot in the photo album, so that I don't forget the things I've seen or learned at certain points. It's hard to believe, sometimes, where I started out or how I got through areas under construction, bumpy sections, or terrible storms. Most journeys are not solo—there are other people with me, or others on the road I interact with, for better or worse; but as I continue along, I'm a changed person. These chapters cover a significant part of Jacob's journey, both physically and spiritually, as the covenant leads him through his life with God.

THE DECEIVER LEARNS A LESSON[1]

Read Genesis 28:10–29:30.

1. God confirms Jacob as the next in line for the covenant in 28:13 – 15. From what we've seen of God so far, what are the chances of his promises becoming reality? According to Jacob's vow in 28:20 – 22, what will determine whether the covenant will continue?

2. Jacob's desires are in line with the covenant goals — he wants Rachel as his wife. But this story looks very different from what we saw a generation ago, when Abraham's servant sought a wife for Isaac in the same place. How does Jacob go about getting a wife? Is he successful? How does God use Jacob's own *modus operandi* to make Jacob's goal harder to achieve?

3. Based on Jacob's previous history, his attitude toward God in Bethel (28:20–22), and his means of working out the plan for his life (29:18–28), how do you think Jacob views God's role in his day-to-day life? How is this attitude similar to that of today's world?

GOING DEEPER

The character flaw to be resolved [in Jacob] goes deeper than the inclination toward deception and manipulation. They are but symptoms of the more pervasive problem of self-sufficiency. We have all met people who do not need anybody or anything. They go through life with the attitude that they can handle anything that comes along. This characteristic is counterproductive to the development of faith.[2]

JACOB'S FAMILY GROWS[3]

Read Genesis 29:31–30:43.

4. Do you ever look up baby names for fun? Scattered among the verses in 29:32–30:24 are explanations for Jacob's children's names (or look for a Bible that explains them in the footnotes). How do their names reflect the tensions in the family? What actions and attitudes do you see repeated from previous generations?

5. Despite the blessing of a growing family, Jacob has his share of problems. First there was the complication of getting Rachel as his wife, then dealing with her infertility; then Jacob must confront the problem of his father-in-law, Laban, manipulating the flocks, adversely affecting Jacob's wealth. How do these problems represent reversals of Jacob's own behavior with Esau?

6. The reversals ooze with irony. Is this just God's sense of humor? What do you suppose God is trying to teach Jacob?

GOING DEEPER

God wants to be recognized as the source of our success. Shrewd or cunning strategies, especially when they involve a level of dishonesty, are counterproductive to God's work in our lives. Just as God negated Jacob's attempts to succeed in order eventually to replace them with his own blessings, God sometimes uses failure in our lives to draw us to depend on him.[4]

PARTING WAYS[5]

Read Genesis 31.

7. What was Jacob's reason(s) for leaving the Promised Land (27:42–44; 28:1–5)? What was his reason(s) for returning to it (31:1–17)? Did he resolve any of his reasons for leaving the Promised Land? Explain.

8. Twenty years is a long time to be away from home. Do you see any evidence of character change in Jacob? What seems to be the same? What seems to be different?

RETURNING TO THE LAND[6]

Read Genesis 32–33.

9. What steps does Jacob take for a peaceful encounter with Esau? What fears remain for Jacob?

GOING DEEPER

On the banks of the River Jabbok, God finally finds Jacob in a situation in which his sense of self-sufficiency is crumbling. Jacob is unable to provide for the security of his family. It is one thing to put yourself in harm's way with the hope that you can find your way out. Jacob has successfully navigated through the maze of rocky relationships with Esau, Laban, and his wives. But in those it was only his own health and welfare hanging in the balance. Now he has his whole family to think about, and he recognizes his inability to vouchsafe their security. This is what finally brings him to his knees.[7]

10. Jacob's wrestling match is a bit hard to imagine, though it paints a powerful picture. It probably encompasses spiritual more than physical struggle.[8] What strengths help Jacob in this encounter? What does he need to let go of?

GOING DEEPER

The nature of Jacob's "prevailing" with God was simply that he held on to God while God weakened him, and wrought in him the spirit of submission and self-distrust; that he had desired God's blessing so much that he clung to God through all this painful humbling, till he came low enough for God to raise him up by speaking peace to him and assuring him that he need not fear about Esau any more.[9]

11. Jacob has no more time to think about his encounter with Esau before Esau arrives. How does Jacob do his best to return everything he "stole" from Esau (33:3, 6–11)? Does this negate the covenant blessing in any way? Explain.

12. Think about your own journey and struggles with God. Are there character qualities in you that God has transformed for his purposes? Are there things you've had to let go of? Would you describe yourself as self-sufficient or God-sufficient?

RESPONDING TO GOD'S WORD

IN YOUR GROUP:

When Jacob encountered God at Bethel, he took the stone from under his head and set it up as a pillar to remember that God was in that place (28:18). Can you think of a place or time that was significant to you—a place you will always remember that you met God there? As time permits, give each person in your group a chance to share such a memory.

ON YOUR OWN:

A few weeks before his death as a missionary in Ecuador, Jim Elliot said, "He is no fool who gives what he cannot keep to gain what he cannot lose."[10] In some ways, I think this characterizes the struggle of Jacob when he finally submitted to God. Are there things that you are still struggling to hold on to that are not really yours to keep? Find a place where you can be alone with God for a while, without distractions, and pray for discernment about things you might be holding on to, such as your self-sufficiency. Finish up your time with a bottle of bubbles! As you blow bubbles into the air, imagine them to be things you need to let go of, then watch them float away from you and disappear.

NOTES

1. This section is based on *NIVAC: Genesis*, 570–587, 595–597.
2. Walton, 611.
3. This section is based on *NIVAC: Genesis*, 587–590, 598–599.
4. Walton, 598.
5. This section is based on *NIVAC: Genesis*, 590–595.
6. This section is based on *NIVAC: Genesis*, 600–621.
7. Walton, 611.
8. Walton, 605.
9. J. I. Packer, *Knowing God* (Downers Grove, Ill.: InterVarsity, 1973), 85. Quoted in Walton, 611.
10. Elisabeth Elliot, *In the Shadow of the Almighty* (New York: Harper, 1958), 15.

SESSION 10

HEARTS THAT WORSHIP

Genesis 34–35; 37–38

Who are you? Without knowing the specifics, I know from Scripture as well as my own experience that you are a person with an active heart—you love, you act, you make decisions (good and bad), you value things and people, and even God himself, based on how your heart has been shaped. I can also pretty much guarantee your family has something to do with the person you have come to be, whether for better or for worse. There's so much we absorb from our families and certain significant experiences that we don't even realize most of the time—although the older I get, the more I see how much of who I am today was shaped in those early formative years. Jacob's family was no different. These chapters reveal how our active hearts make themselves known in the actions of our day-to-day lives.

PASSIONS OVERFLOW IN SHECHEM[1]

Read Genesis 34.

1. When Abram was first called by God to leave his home and go to a place God would choose, his first stop in Canaan was Shechem. God told Abram that he would give this land to Abram's offspring, and Abram built an altar to the Lord in response (12:5–7). What do you think Abram would think of his offspring, just three generations later in the same place?

2. It's not entirely clear from the text whether Dinah was opposed to Shechem's advances. It's conceivable that it was a ruse to bypass an arranged marriage.[2] Shechem was certainly persistent in pursuing marriage with Dinah and ignored accepted boundaries to make her his own (34:7). Jacob's sons were justifiably furious over the event, but inexcusably violent by anyone's standards. To borrow language from the book of Judges, they seem to all be doing what's right in their own eyes — Shechem, Jacob's sons, and possibly even Dinah. In the end, the covenant continues to advance — the Israelites do not intermarry with the Canaanites. Does the end justify the means? Is this a way you would expect God to overcome a potential covenant obstacle? Explain.

3. Circumcision was first introduced as a confirmation of the covenant with God when Abraham was ninety-nine years old. What motivated him to get circumcised (17:1–14)? What motivated Jacob's sons to tell Shechem to be circumcised (34:13–15, 25)? Why did Shechem do it (34:19)? What motivated the other men of the city to follow suit (34:21–24)? What does this reveal about the hearts of each of these people?

WORSHIP IN THE HOUSE OF GOD[3]

Read Genesis 35.

The second stop in Abram's journey in Canaan was Bethel ("House of God"). Jacob's family seems to be walking in Abram's footsteps — from Paddan Aram, where Abram's extended family still lived, to Shechem, and then to Bethel.

4. When God first called Abram (12:1), he had to leave behind his country, his people, and his father's household, which, as we noted in session 4, included his father's household gods.4 Jacob's sons are asked to do a similar thing in this chapter, and they do bury the foreign gods they probably collected at Shechem (35:2–4). But think back to Jacob prior to wrestling with God at the Jabbok River (32:22–32). What defined Jacob's actions in the early part of his life, or to put it another way, what was the "god" that motivated Jacob (32:28)? What evidence is there that Jacob's sons have not abandoned their father's former "god" (34:13, 25–29)? What would it actually mean for Jacob's sons to leave behind their father's former gods?

GOING DEEPER

Burying idols (35:4) is not the same as destroying them. In fact, the text more precisely says that Jacob hides them, not that he buries them. The Hebrew verb used is the same one used when Achan hides the spoils he took from Jericho by burying them in his tent (Josh. 7:21–22).5

5. On the surface, Genesis 35 seems like a climax for the covenant. What events would you count as advances for the covenant (see 35:4, 7, 8, 9–15, 18, 19, 27, 29)? Now consider the surrounding context. Jacob's sons are involved in activities that don't exactly qualify as godly: destroying the inhabitants of Shechem (ch. 34), selling off Joseph to traders headed for Egypt (ch. 37), marrying Canaanite women and then consorting with a temple prostitute (ch. 38). What might the actions of Jacob's sons in the surrounding chapters (chs. 34, 37, 38) suggest about the sincerity of their hearts in worship at Bethel, the House of God (ch. 35)? Do you see any parallels today in discrepancies between daily living and worship in the church? (See also Matt. 7:17–20; James 2:14–26.)

6. Before we move on completely from Shechem, let's take one more look at its significance for the Israelites who heard this story when they were on the verge of entering the Promised Land under Joshua's leadership. Eventually, they will gather in Shechem again. Read Joshua 24, particularly verses 1–3 and 14–15. What similarities do you see between Jacob's generation and Joshua's generation? How does the challenge those generations faced continue even today?

FAMILY DIVISION[6]

Read Genesis 37.

7. It seems a bit odd, when you think about it, that Jacob's sons, who acted so zealously in defense of their sister Dinah (ch. 34), would act so treacherously against their brother Joseph. It suggests family loyalty wasn't their only motivating factor. Take a little closer look at the family dynamics that might have been in play in 29:32–35; 34:1, 25; 37:3–4, 18–28. What could be fueling the brothers' anger toward Joseph (on top of his dreams)?

8. Of all the brothers, Reuben seems to be the only one looking out for Joseph's welfare (37:21–22, 29–30). What possible motivation could he have for coming to Joseph's aid (see 35:22 and 49:1–4)?

9. In the well-known conclusion of Joseph's story, he tells his brothers, "You intended to harm me, but God intended it for good to accomplish what is now being done, the saving of many lives" (50:20). What providential events (i.e., seemingly by chance) in Genesis 37 point to the fact that God was already working out his plan for Joseph even before his brothers began plotting his destruction?

ANOTHER MASQUERADE[7]

Read Genesis 38.

10. Whether he knows it or not, in what ways is Judah acting counter to the covenant in Genesis 38?

GOING DEEPER

Levirate marriage laws required that if a woman's husband died without offspring having been produced, it was the duty of his brother to bear a child by her in order to continue his dead brother's line. This custom is established as legislation in the Mosaic law (Deut. 25:5–10) but also is evidenced in the broader culture by its inclusion among Hittite laws.... Hittite law regarding levirate marriage stipulates that when a widow marries her late husband's brother, if he dies, she is then to marry his father (i.e., her father-in-law).[8]

11. Masquerades have been woven throughout Jacob's extended family history. How does Tamar use a masquerade to her advantage? How would Jacob's family have been different if it weren't for masquerades?

12. Look at Jesus' genealogy in Matthew 1:1–16. Creation wasn't the only time when God had to work miracles to establish his kingdom! What obstacles did God overcome in each of the generations listed in Matthew 1:2–3b? Why was it so important? What does this tell you about God?

RESPONDING TO GOD'S WORD

IN YOUR GROUP:

What would you say is something significant that was passed down from your family to you? How does it impact your daily life?

ON YOUR OWN:

How well do you know your family tree? Besides other legacies that may have been passed on, can you trace back the attitude of faith that other generations in your family had? If you can, interview an older person in your family to learn more and write it down to pass on to others.

NOTES

1. This section is based on *NIVAC: Genesis*, 622–630, 633–635.
2. Walton, 628.
3. This section is based on *NIVAC: Genesis*, 630–633, 635–640.
4. Walton, 392.
5. Walton, 631.
6. This section is based on *NIVAC: Genesis*, 662–666, 688–690, 694–695.
7. This section is based on *NIVAC: Genesis*, 666–670, 690–691.
8. Walton, 667–668.

A BLESSED NATION

Genesis 39 – 41

There's a certain "genre" in children's songs which involves remembering a long string of events that all build on one another somewhat unpredictably—"The Old Lady Who Swallowed a Fly," "The Twelve Days of Christmas," "The Bump on the Log in the Hole on the Bottom of the Sea," "The Hole in the Bucket," "The Austrian Who Went Yodeling"—you could probably add your own favorites. The challenge, of course, is to remember everything in order as the story builds. Did you ever consider the fact that the style of such far-out stories is actually anchored in biblical tradition? Truth is stranger than fiction, and the way God strings together characters and details in his own story (and ours) is an amazing testimony of his sovereignty and grace. Joseph's story is certainly an example of that.

JOSEPH BRINGS GOD'S BLESSING[1]

Read Genesis 39:1–20a.

1. The scene of God's covenant story now shifts to Joseph in Egypt. This is certainly not the first time someone in Abraham's line has interacted with other nations, even Egypt. How did God show his covenant blessing in those situations (12:16–20; 20:14–18; 26:11–16; 30:40–43)? How has the blessing shifted in 39:1–5? Is this consistent with the covenant promises? Explain.

2. Both Judah (Gen. 38) and Joseph were separated from the rest of their brothers for a time. How were their experiences different from one another? Think especially about their freedom of choice, their blessings, their attitudes toward God, and the results of their interactions with women.

3. Now think about the same question, but compare Joseph and Adam. Obviously the circumstances were different, but God put both of them in places where they were blessed with everything they could possibly need, with restrictions on just one thing—for Adam, the Tree of Knowledge; for Joseph, Potiphar's wife. How were their experiences different from one another? Think especially about their freedom of choice, their blessings, their attitudes toward God, and the results of their interactions with women. Has the covenant made a difference in humanity's understanding of God?

SUCCESS IN UNLIKELY PLACES[2]

Read Genesis 39:20b–40:23.

4. Things seem to be going from bad to worse—Joseph is sold into slavery by his brothers, he's unjustly accused of fooling around with his master's wife, and now he's stuck in prison with no end in sight. What evidence is there that God is still working in Joseph's behalf even in the prison?

5. If you were in Joseph's shoes, it would be pretty easy to be depressed at this point. However, there's no indication that Joseph is in despair. What difference does it make to look at Joseph's circumstances through eyes of faith versus eyes of doubt? If you already know the end of the story, how does that help you to see things differently?

6. How do we view our circumstances affects how we act in them. Although God is clearly orchestrating the details in this story, Joseph's actions are important as well. Despite his circumstances, what steps of faith does Joseph take to coincide with God's work in the prison? How does God honor these steps?

GOING DEEPER

In the ancient Near East, dream interpretations were sought from experts who had been trained in techniques and methods of the day. Both the Egyptians and Babylonians compiled what are called "dream books," which contain sample dreams along with a key to their interpretation. Though some of the interpretations in the biblical accounts may seem transparent or self-evident, dreams often depended on symbolism, and the symbols might not stand for what was most logical. . . . Joseph was not familiar with any of the "scientific" literature and would not have had access to it, so he consulted God. Regardless, his interpretation follows the way the dream literature interpreted comparable symbols.[3]

JOSEPH IN CHARGE OF EGYPT[4]

Read Genesis 41.

7. As in the prison, God's actions work hand in hand with Joseph's to accomplish his purposes. What circumstances in this chapter point clearly to God's handiwork? How does Joseph step up to the plate?

8. It's one thing for Joseph to recognize God's handiwork and give him credit. It's another for the Egyptians to learn more about Joseph's God. How does God make use of the Egyptian culture and environment to communicate his supreme power? What evidence is there that God successfully gets his message across?

GOING DEEPER

Certainly any deity who could foist such a severe famine on Egypt must be a powerful one. Egypt does not depend on rainfall for its food production but on the flooding of the Nile, which is much more dependable. Rarely, then, did the country suffer extended famine. The gods connected to the Nile and its annual flooding were considered to be powerful gods, who would have to be restrained in some way (or angered by some offense) for the inundation to fail for seven years.[5]

9. Pharaoh wastes no time putting Joseph in charge, even though it was unusual at that time to give a non-Egyptian so much power.[6] How is Joseph's new role similar to his role in Potiphar's house and in the prison? How is it different?

10. The choice of language by the author of Genesis reminds us that the God of creation in chapter 1 is the same as the God who rules the nations in chapter 41. When Pharaoh recognizes the spirit of God in Joseph (41:38), it is the same word that describes the Spirit of God hovering over the waters in 1:2.[7] Four times, the author confirms that things turn out exactly as Joseph said they would (40:22; 41:13, 28, 54), reminiscent of God's language at the end of each day of creation. Back in the first chapter of Genesis, John Walton said this of human existence: "Being made in the image of God confers on us *dignity*, entrusts us with *responsibility*, and implants in us a certain potential, namely, the *capacity* to mirror our Creator."[8]

How does Joseph reflect the image of God in all that he does? In the end, would you describe him as Pharaoh's man or God's man? Explain.

On the surface, Joseph is being "made" by Pharaoh. Everything he is given comes from Pharaoh's hand: his office, status, privilege, name, wife—everything. He is "reborn" as a servant of Pharaoh. The irony is that from the standpoint of Genesis, it is not the hand of Pharaoh that has remade Joseph but the hand of God. For all that Pharaoh did, God brought Joseph to the recognition of Pharaoh, and God gave Joseph wisdom and success. In the end, Joseph is not first and foremost Pharaoh's man, but God's man. He is not Pharaoh's instrument of economic survival; he is God's instrument of salvation.[9]

GOING DEEPER

11. Our role in redemptive history is obviously not the same as Joseph's. And yet we also are made in God's image, called to live as his people. How does Joseph's life challenge you to view the circumstances in which God has placed you? How are you doing as God's image-bearer?

12. Joseph's life points us to the greatest image-bearer of all—Jesus Christ. More than anyone, Jesus acted faithfully through humbling circumstances and was raised to a position of great honor and responsibility in order to save his people. God's Spirit was in him, and everything turned out exactly as he said it would, including his death and resurrection. How can understanding the complexities and victories of different people in God's story give you hope in your own story?

RESPONDING TO GOD'S WORD

IN YOUR GROUP:

How well do you know God's story? See how long you can go around in a circle and have each person add a phrase to the sentence, "God created the earth, which led to the creation of man, which led to . . ." culminating in God's people worshiping him in heaven for eternity.

ON YOUR OWN:

Think about your own personal story. What people, books, and events, good or bad, on purpose or inadvertently, led you to the understanding you have of God right now? Take time to thank God for the ways in which he has led you toward him, even the difficult things.

NOTES

1. This section is based on *NIVAC: Genesis*, 670–672, 692–696.
2. This section is based on *NIVAC: Genesis*, 672–673.
3. Walton, 672–673.
4. This section is based on *NIVAC: Genesis*, 673–677, 691, 694.
5. Walton, 675.
6. Walton, 677.
7. Walton, 676.
8. Walton, 137, italics original.
9. Walton, 691.

A NEW BEGINNING

Genesis 42–50

I cannot count the number of times while reading that I've either thought or said to someone, "I'll stop when I get to the end of this chapter," and then found I had to go on "just a little more." I think one sign of a great book is cliff-hanger chapter endings—the circumstances of the chapter are pretty much resolved, but then something else happens and you've just *got* to keep going. I think Genesis is a bit like that. A lot has been revealed about the nature of God; the covenant family is quite firmly established despite numerous obstacles; the nature of humankind has become a bit clearer; then all of a sudden the covenant family is whisked off somewhere else. This is just the beginning of God's story, with a lot of twists and turns still coming, and much more to say about the nature of God and humanity. Hopefully it will make you hungry for the next chapter, and the next.

JOSEPH TESTS HIS BROTHERS[1]

Read Genesis 42–44.

1. Masquerades have been a theme in the life of Jacob's family. What does God begin to reveal to Joseph when his brothers don't recognize him (42:8–9)? By not revealing his identity, what does Joseph learn about the family he has not seen for twenty-two years (42:13, 21–22)?

2. Joseph now engages in the most elaborate masquerade of all to test the hearts of his brothers. In the first part of his plan, he holds on to one of the brothers (42:19, 24). In the second test, he shows favoritism to Benjamin, then lets them all go, but sets up Benjamin to be potentially abandoned by the other brothers to slavery (43:33–44:2, 10). How will Joseph's elaborate scheme reveal to him if his brothers have changed?

3. The author uses a series of incidents to point out how completely the roles have reversed for Joseph and his brothers. Compare the following verses and note what has changed:

a. Genesis 37:2, 14 with 42:9

b. Genesis 37:18 – 20 with 42:17 – 19, 30

c. Genesis 37:25, 28 with 43:11 – 13

d. Genesis 37:26 – 27 with 44:33

e. Genesis 37:31 – 35 with 44:30 – 32, 34

4. Compare 37:14 with 43:26 – 27. In what respect has Joseph's role remained consistent toward his brothers? What has he found out? Do you think his brothers have changed their ways?

 GOING DEEPER

[I]t becomes clear that Judah (presumably with the rest of the brothers) has become altruistic. He would rather bear slavery than blame. He is selflessly willing to accept his own misery rather than put others in misery. This transformation of the brothers represented in Judah is every bit as miraculous as the transformation in the status of Joseph. [2]

MOVING TO EGYPT [3]

Read Genesis 45:1 – 46:7 and 46:28 – 47:12.

5. Joseph ends his masquerade by stunning his brothers with his true identity. How does Joseph's perspective on God transform Israel's understanding of God's sovereignty (45:4 – 11)?

6. What other events point to the fact that the sojourn to Egypt by Israel and his extended family is part of God's plan, and not a "plan B" when things went wrong (15:12 – 16; 37:5 – 9; 41:28 – 32; 46:1 – 4)?

7. What aspects of God's covenant are fulfilled by moving to Egypt (46:3 – 4; 47:7, 10, 11 – 12)?

8. The original audience hearing Genesis has a rather low view of Egypt, having just escaped from slavery and harsh treatment there. How can Joseph's lesson about God's purposes help them to see their own experiences in Egypt differently?

GOING DEEPER

God's sovereignty and blessing can be found in what appear to be the most heinous crimes and the most disastrous circumstances. This does not mean that God approves of the crimes or that he enjoys bringing disaster into our lives. It is simply a testimony to his ability to bring good out of evil. The depths of God's sovereignty are not demonstrated by his repression of our choices that inevitably reveal our sinfulness and fallen self-will, but by the fact that there is no choice that we can make, however sinful or fallen, that can interfere with his plan. In fact, often enough, as in the case of Joseph, those choices end up furthering his plan.[4]

A NEW GENERATION[5]

Read Genesis 47:13–49:1 and 49:29–50:26.

9. What influence does Joseph have on Egypt during the years of famine (47:14–15, 18–19, 25)? How is he regarded by the Egyptians? How are the Israelites affected during that time (47:27)?

10. How does Jacob influence the course of events for the next generation of Israelites (48:5–6, 12–20)? For all the preferential treatment Joseph has had from Jacob over his life, what legacy does Jacob leave to Joseph?

11. Joseph weeps when he finds out that his brothers are still afraid of him after Jacob's death. They are still bearing the guilt of what they did to Joseph close to forty years after they sold him into slavery (50:17). What does this reveal about the power of guilt? How does it point to the need for more than mere explanations to cleanse the effects of wrongdoing?

12. How does Joseph's understanding that God can bring good out of harmful intents (50:20) summarize what has happened in Genesis as a whole? Genesis ends with the covenant family identified as a distinct people, flourishing and provided for, blessed and blessing other nations. On one level, God has fulfilled his promises to them. But they are in Egypt, not in the land that God promised them, with Joseph's bones waiting to be buried, and the promise that God will surely come to their aid. How does God's revelation in Genesis give both the original readers and us assurance that he will overcome this and all future obstacles?

GOING DEEPER

God has shown his mastery in creation, covenant, and history.... [A]ll of this is just the beginning. The biblical narratives continue to pursue this quest through the history of Israel as well as theologically through the redemptive history that culminates in the work of Christ. Salvation shows God's mastery over the chaos that came about because of sin. Eventually all chaos will be subdued as God establishes his kingdom forever and the forces of chaos are finally destroyed, not just balanced, limited, or contained.[6]

RESPONDING TO GOD'S WORD

IN YOUR GROUP:

There have been quite a few parallels pointed out between Joseph, who saved his people (and the people of Egypt) from starvation, and Jesus, who saved humanity from sin. See how many parallels you can come up with as a group.

ON YOUR OWN:

Can you think of examples in your own life where harm was intended but God brought good out of it? Take time to thank God for the gracious ways he has worked in your life.

NOTES

1. This section is based on *NIVAC: Genesis*, 677–682, 694–696.
2. Walton, 681–682.
3. This section is based on *NIVAC: Genesis*, 682–688, 696–702.
4. Walton, 696.
5. This section is based on *NIVAC: Genesis*, 703–727.
6. Walton, 724.

LEADER'S NOTES

SESSION 1 LEADER'S NOTES

1. The Israelites descended from Abraham, who originally came from Mesopotamia. In Moses' time, the Israelites had the added influence of Egypt, since they had been in slavery there for hundreds of years. They would primarily be concerned with their most basic needs: food, water, and shelter. Following closely behind that would be protection — both from natural calamities such as weather, predators, and disease, as well as from enemies, leading to questions about life and death, and who was in control of all those things.

2. There is clear support in Scripture for our belief that God made all matter in the cosmos, and that he made it out of nothing. The apostle Paul's letter to the Romans claims that this is obvious to anyone who looks at creation, unless they are suppressing that information. Many psalms also point to God's creation. But creation *ex nihilo* is basically a presupposition of Scripture rather than something that is proven by Scripture.

3. The visualization of the beginning as dark, chaotic, and formless in 1:1–2 is very similar to the mythology of the ancient Near East and would make sense to the people hearing it. However, the naming of God as someone distinct from the creation and in charge of the creation, hovering over it, is a very different view from that of the elements themselves taking on godlike characteristics.

4. "The face value of Genesis 1:3–5 does not offer a description of the piece of our material cosmos that physicists know as light with all of its physical properties and functional operation. What carries much more importance for the biblical author and in the ancient world in general is the affirmation that [by creating the days] God created time."[1]

   Time is such an integral part of our lives, it is hard to imagine a world without it—it is integral to the way in which we organize and measure our lives.

5. Each day begins with "And God said," pointing to God's creation and ordering simply by speaking a command. Each of these statements is followed by "And it was so," further emphasizing God's power—whatever he commands happens. He also describes each day as good. This gives all of creation a positive value ascribed by God, which is different from other mythologies which described some of the elements as evil.

6. On day two, the sky is formed, which is the source of all of our weather.[2] On day three, dry land and seas are separated, and then vegetation is produced. From a functional approach, these elements are closely related to agriculture.[3] These elements are critical to the survival of the Israelites, and all agrarian-based cultures who depend on the local land for food.

7. The basic elements that have been created so far—time, weather, and agriculture—are what determine life and death, both then and now. They are a source of blessing, but also of struggle. Major devastation is caused when conditions are wrong for a fruitful land, even with all the technological advances we've made. It's a reminder that we are dependent on God—always.

8. God fills his day and night with celestial bodies (days one and four); he populates the sky and waters with birds and fish (days two and five); and he populates the dry land with animals and people (days three and six). He has organized and filled his realm to his perfect satisfaction.

9. We wrongly exploit this belief when we see the world as ours to use or misuse as we please. Instead of managers or stewards of God's creation, we view ourselves as owners and strip it for our own personal gain. Conversely, we sometimes hold animal life in higher esteem than human life, whether in pouring endless resources into saving whales when genocide or infanticide is occurring, or honoring the ape as much as the human.

In creating humankind in God's image, God gave us dignity as well as responsibility in a world that revolves around him, not us.

10. God's creation is bursting with life and order, and the people made in his image are expected to carry on the work that God began. The development of civilization points to how this begins to happen. Unfortunately, we have been much more successful in filling the world than governing and managing it effectively.

11. The Bible describes God as the one sovereign ruler for all time, seated at the throne of his completed universe. All of the cosmos is his, with the earth as a footstool on which to rest his feet. In Hebrews, Jesus is described as the high priest who serves in God's heavenly sanctuary, which is dimly reflected in the sanctuary on earth. It clearly puts God in the center of the universe, not us. Jesus' seat at God's right hand is another image that points to the divinity of Christ.

12. This question is not about style of worship or Sabbath regulations. We need to recognize the privilege we have to enter God's presence at all, based on the forgiveness of sins we have received through the sacrifice of Jesus on the cross. And we need to recognize our dependence on God, the author and ruler of all things, and worship him with our whole hearts in thanksgiving.

NOTES

1. Walton, 84.
2. See Walton, 110–113.
3. Walton, 113.

1. We are told in Genesis 2:8–10 that the Lord planted a garden, put all kinds of pleasing trees in it, good for food and pleasing to the eye, and that it was watered by a river flowing from Eden. Then he put Adam, and subsequently his helper, Eve, in the garden to tend it. It fits the description of a successful king who lives adjacent to the garden, ruling from his palace.

2. *My* thoughts on Paradise tend to revolve around sunny beaches, turquoise waters, and palm trees (and being served hand and foot). The reality described in Genesis was much more God-centered. In fact, the sense of "Paradise Lost" for the ancient Israelite was focused on the loss of God's presence with them, not creature comforts.[1] By putting Adam and Eve in the garden, he gave them protection, access to himself, the ability to produce food, and the capability of reproducing—all that was entailed in the blessing. By bringing living creatures to the man to name, God allowed Adam to exercise his authority over them.[2]

3. In the Bible, humankind is called to work on behalf of and even alongside of God to accomplish his purposes, rather than be a slave to him. There is no drudgery in work until after the fall. Women are seen as helpers in the human endeavor, not just as reproductive organs. In both men and women, what is being produced benefits them directly—they are blessed by the food they can eat; their marriage is to one another, not to the gods for their pleasure. The God of Israel has no needs that must be fulfilled for him to survive. This is a much higher view of humankind (and more enjoyable too!) than in the surrounding cultures.

4. Obedience and wisdom are different things. Even children of very young ages can be taught obedience and the consequences of disobedience without understanding everything behind it. God clearly told Adam that this tree was forbidden, or else death was sure. He and Eve are responsible.

5. God was quite clear about exactly which tree not to eat from and what the consequences were for disobedience (2:16–17). The serpent begins to alter God's words by asking about "any tree," which Eve corrects, but not completely; adding to God's words by saying they couldn't touch it either. The serpent's flat-out lie comes when he denies the consequence of death. He

plays mind games with Eve, tempting her with the benefits of knowledge, temptations to which she succumbs. Perhaps she thought it was similar enough to the other trees that it would be okay to eat. Or, having been made in the image of God, perhaps she thought becoming more like him was not a bad thing. At any rate, she serves herself rather than God in this action, listening to a creature rather than the Creator despite all of his provisions for them so far.

6. Bottom line: God is more trustworthy than any other sources. We remain dependent on him regardless of our choices, but as we will see in the next section, things can get much more difficult when we try to operate independently. Any time a desire becomes more important than obeying God, we have to look carefully at what (or who) it is we serve. Eve desired knowledge more than obedience—she was serving herself, not God in that moment. Romans 1:18–25 warns against exchanging the truth of God for a lie, and consequently worshiping and serving created things (including ourselves) rather than the Creator. That's exactly what Eve did.

7. Shame enters the picture immediately, as Adam and Eve become aware of their nakedness and cover themselves. Then they hide from God because they're afraid of him. In responding to God's questions, both Adam and Eve blame someone else rather than taking responsibility for their actions. Unfortunately, shame, strife, anxiety, distrust, blame—the typical fruits of evil—still characterize our relationships with God and with one another, evidence of the evil that continues to "crouch at our door" (see Gen. 4:7) when we fail to do the right thing.

8. The blessing is not revoked, but it gets a whole lot harder to carry out, outside of the protected, well-watered garden. The serpent and the ground are cursed. The woman's pain and anxiety surrounding childbearing are greatly increased—possibly connected to (1) the fact that she knows her children will face enmity from the offspring of the serpent, (2) the difficulty of producing food, and (3) the certainty of death.[3] The man's ability to produce food, the other aspect of God's blessing, is greatly compromised because of the curse on the ground.

9. The fact that this is the beginning of the story, not the end, points to a long-term plan of God that will take many generations to carry out. God's blessing is just beginning, even if Adam and Eve have made it harder on

themselves. More specifically, God clothed them and, in the traditional view, prevented them from access to the Tree of Life so they would not be stuck in their sinful state eternally. The Tree of Life reappears in Revelation 22:2 and 22:14 for the benefit of those worthy to eat it.[4]

10. A new generation is born to Eve, and their crops and flocks seem to be flourishing—evidence of God's blessing on the family. However, Cain's anger and jealousy, resulting in murder and defensiveness, are clearly evidence of sin that Cain is unable to master. Like the previous generation, God questions Cain who takes no responsibility for his actions. Although Cain is punished, God's grace is evident through the protection he offers Cain.

11. Answers could include such things as the loss of God's presence, the grace and patience God shows despite humankind's sin, the loss of innocence in humankind, the difficulty of post-fall work compared to pre-fall, the speed of the descent of sin, the incredible sorrow in God's story, the need for a savior, etc.

12. God declared that this world is good. Everything that he declared in Genesis 1 came to be, so we can trust that it is still so, even though it might not always be evident. His grace is at work from the very beginning, giving us hope even when we are disobedient. At the same time, he does not falter in carrying out punishment and consequences when necessary—a good thing to remember when we experience evil. Just because God's creation has fallen into sin, it does not mean that his reign has ended. He continues to rule from his throne, resting from his work over an abundant kingdom that will ultimately be at peace.

NOTES

1. Walton, 231.
2. Walton, 178.
3. Walton, 238–239.
4. For further discussion of an alternative view that the Tree of Life was the means for human beings to avoid death even before the fall, see Walton, 183–185.

SESSION 3 LEADER'S NOTES

1. God was grieved over the state of the world (6:5–7), but he was not annoyed like the gods in the Near Eastern accounts. After weighing the actions of his creation, God found them wanting and judged them. The supreme and powerful ruler is at the helm, with all the forces of the earth at his command. At the same time, his mercy was extended to the one family that was righteous.

2. Noah's account is really about God and his continuing control of the earth. Out of chaos, God brings new order—what he commands still happens. There is a sense of new beginnings, starting with a wind hovering over the waters, similar to the Spirit of 1:2, followed by God filling the earth again with all his creatures.

3. The emotions describing God are grief and pain, not anger and vengeance. God's judgment is more like controlled discipline than unleashed anger. Even as he destroys the rest of the world, he makes allowance for a remnant, even knowing that humankind's heart would not be changed by the experience (8:21). His grace is evident in the creation of the ark, and his covenant with Noah for future blessing.

4. When we become Christians, Christ himself takes on the judgment that should have been ours. But we don't come out of it unchanged. God begins a refining process of judging the stuff in us that needs to die, and bringing new life out of the ashes. He transforms us into the people we were meant to be, often through difficult experiences he puts us through. That's why we shouldn't shy away from struggles (James 1:2). In response to his work in us, God calls us to give our lives as sacrificial gifts that are pleasing to him (Rom. 12:1).

5. *The blessing* is virtually the same in both accounts, except for the fear factor of the animals, which may be accounted for as a natural response to the new hunting options (Gen. 9:2–3). *Food provision* for people expands to animal as well as plant life. This probably refers to game, since domestic flocks were already around, though they were probably used primarily for milk and hair/wool.[1] There was a *prohibition* against eating fruit from the Tree of Knowledge in Genesis 2. In Genesis 9 eating meat with its lifeblood still in it was forbidden. Essentially this was a way of asking

God's permission for his bounty, and respectfully returning the life force of the animal to him. No comparable prohibition is known elsewhere in the ancient world.[2] *Filling the earth* is made possible in Genesis 2 by creating Eve. In Genesis 9, God pledges never to destroy life like he did in the flood, so he would not be counteracting his own blessing. Adam and Eve give into *temptation* by the serpent in the garden (crossing a food boundary). Ham tempts his brothers to look at his father's nakedness in Genesis 9 (a reproduction boundary), but Shem and Japheth resist, covering their father instead. In Genesis 3, God *curses* the serpent and the ground, and makes it harder for Adam and Eve to carry out the blessing. Noah's curse on Canaan is not nearly as binding, since he is not God, but is clearly meant to have repercussions on Ham's clan. This would have great significance for the original audience, who were on the verge of taking over the land of Canaan.

6. The flood provides a sobering reality check on the new world. The blessing continues, with even greater freedom than before. But with that freedom comes responsibility—respecting the life of every living creature, which gives people a charge to carry out justice. God has made it abundantly clear that he cares deeply about justice and righteousness and will enforce his standards.

7. Instead of weighing the sin of humanity as a whole, God's vow (9:11) shifts justice toward the righteousness (or lack thereof) of the individual. His demand for the accounting of lifeblood, especially of people, puts more responsibility for justice in the hands of people, imperfect though they are—not just himself.

8. It seems pretty risky for God to put justice in the hands of imperfect humans. But by having greater "ownership" for our deeds and misdeeds, we should value life more and become better skilled at carrying out justice. Unfortunately, we are still fallible when it comes to administering justice, as is clear from mistaken convictions and failing correctional systems. Capital punishment is a volatile issue today, although Walton argues for the continuing need for it despite our errors.[3] Christians should continue to think through and be involved in carrying out our justice despite its difficulties.

9. The ultimate "fresh start" came in the form of God's Son, Jesus, who took on a punishment for universal sin that was on the scale of the flood, even though we are the ones who deserve it. This was the only thing that could break the cycle of sin in human lives, since we couldn't do it on our own. Because of his ongoing forgiveness, we can start fresh on a regular basis, being purified as white as snow (Isa. 1:18).

10. Instead of human beings made in God's image and placed in God's garden for his service, God is being made in the image of a human being and placed in society for its service. It is a complete reversal of the ordained order that reduces God to what the people wanted him to be.

11. I think this comes out most clearly in our prayer life, when it becomes a string of requests. Sometimes we try to negotiate with God, promising something we'll do in return for his blessing or service. We act as if God is our puppet, though we would never put it that way. When we do such things, God is no longer God—he is a figment of our own creation.

12. "When the concept of God becomes as distorted as it has by Genesis 11, the only path to reclaim humanity is for God to reveal himself anew."[4] God scatters the people so that they can't continue to build on each other's ideas and multiply evil in the process. Then he chooses one group through which to make himself known, beginning with Abraham, the subject of our next session.

NOTES

1. Walton, 341–342.
2. Walton, 343.
3. Walton, 356–358.
4. Walton, 382.

SESSION 4 LEADER'S NOTES

1. At this point in the story of redemption, God chooses Abram specifically to be the one from whom he creates a great nation, and God promises to bless the other peoples of the world through him. God chooses Abram in order to make himself and his purposes more clearly known to one group of people, who then will be expected to "translate" God's purposes to the world.

2. Abram's blessing is already at risk because of Sarai's infertility. He gives up all security when he leaves—the land, his family, his inheritance, and whatever gods he's accustomed to worshiping. It doesn't make sense from a human perspective. But God is promising Abram much more—new land, developing into a great nation (implying offspring), blessing and protection, and even blessing others beyond his own family. It's a risky step, but with the expectation that God will follow through on his promises, it's a step for the better.

3. In the garden, blessing was at Adam and Eve's fingertips—food everywhere, and Eve created to be the mother of all. After the fall, life became more painful, but there was still evidence of growth and provision—crops, flocks and families growing. Now, the stakes seem higher. Abram must believe God and wait to see the promises fulfilled—there's more of a future orientation to the blessing. Things might look bad for Abram right now, but he's beginning to learn more about God in the process, which in the long run is a better thing.

4. The famine itself is a challenge to the blessing. While it's understandable for Abram to head to better land, it means leaving the land God gave him. Morality aside, Sarai joining Pharaoh's harem further compromises any hope of establishing a great nation in Abram's name. It would seem that God's promises of blessing are on the verge of collapse.

5. Regardless of whether Abram's actions in Egypt were right or wrong, God uses them to bless Abram. The Egyptians *did* treat Abram well for Sarai's sake, so he accumulated significant wealth in the way of livestock and servants. God also inflicted diseases on the Egyptians, causing Abram to be sent back to the Promised Land with all that he had accumulated. God

is clearly in charge of all the details that happen in all nations, even while he allows individuals to make choices for themselves.

6. Abram lets Lot decide where to settle, but by his own choice, Lot leaves Canaan to Abram while he heads east. Canaan might not have looked as good to human eyes, but it is the land of God's blessing. Lot has chosen to head east, which in past stories has typically been a move away from God (3:24; 4:16; 11:2), toward a city that the original readers would start shaking their heads over as soon as it was mentioned.

7. The text says nothing about this decision being right or wrong. If anything, Lot seems to have made a wise choice based on the availability of water. Many decisions we make are not between "sinful" and "righteous" options. We just have to make the best decision we can, and trust God for the results.

8. "For many of us ... the real obstacle is not something external but internal. Sometimes the obstacle is simply the routines of life that have bound us to a particular status quo.... Dare we pray that the Lord might remove or overcome these obstacles that may be preventing us from taking the next step in our spiritual growth or interfering with God's work and blessing in our lives? God is willing and able."[1]

9. Unlike the other kings who were fighting to gain or defend their territory, Abram only got involved when his nephew Lot was in trouble, but he was prepared with the resources to defend his family. He had trained men whom he was able to divide up to attack and defeat the enemy, safely getting back Lot as well as the other people and goods that were involved.

10. Abram's victory puts him in a position to gain power and dominion in the area, which would certainly seem to promote his "great nation" status, even though his intent was only to save his nephew. In some ways, it's the best of both worlds — he gains respect of other leaders in the area, but in a way that isn't domineering.

11. Although Abram is aware of God's promises, he seems willing to wait on God's timing to make them happen — he doesn't seize opportunities or goods for himself. Adam and Eve, by contrast, took active steps toward their own advancement — and suffered disastrous consequences.

12. Every situation needs to be considered carefully to determine the wisdom of seizing versus waiting. God often accomplishes his goals for us in ways

that we would never expect, with timing that we would not anticipate. One key principle we can learn from Abram is whether our actions are self-directed or God-directed. Input from others and God's Word can help us discern the right direction to go, but ultimately submission to God's Spirit is necessary to step in the right direction. Fortunately, as we saw in the beginning of this session, whether we move in the right or wrong direction, God has the ability to use our decisions, right or wrong, to lead us in the direction he wants.

NOTE

1. Walton, 434.

SESSION 5 LEADER'S NOTES

1. God begins with a general statement, that he is Abram's shield and great reward (15:1). But then he is much more specific, addressing Abram's concerns, stating that he will have a direct heir and offspring as numerous as the stars (15:4 – 5). He reminds Abram that he is the one who brought him to Canaan from Ur and gave the land to him (15:7). God promises Abram something that humanly speaking was impossible, something only God himself could do. And Abram takes God at his word (15:6), demonstrating that he believes God has the power to do exactly what he says. This is analogous in the New Testament to Christian faith that believes in the resurrection as evidence of God's saving grace and power, something that is humanly impossible. Abram then asks for more clarification (15:8). Asking for more specifics does not mean that he doubted God, so these are not contradictory.

2. God is taking on the "problem" of reproduction in both cases, coming up with creative solutions that only he could manage both times — creating Eve as a helper, then promising an heir to Abram that only he could produce. Both solutions are "conceived" in a state of deep sleep (2:21; 15:12). Abram, unlike Adam, questioned God, looking for an answer to a problem he could not see an answer to. God's response to Abram points to a solution in the future requiring Abram's trust, unlike Adam who woke up to see Eve in front of him.

3. "Faith is being sure of what we hope for and certain of what we do not see" (Heb. 11:1). There are many times when trust involves accepting details different from what we expected, or timing that was not our first choice. Underlying such faith is a belief that God ultimately has our good in mind, even if he defines that good differently than we would. Hopefully, such moments cause us to lean on God all the more and to seek him out as Abram did. Trusting God comes easier when we have some history of his work in our lives or others' lives — Abram was just beginning to see that; we have the privilege of having the Bible to look back at God's faithfulness throughout history, as well as instances in our personal lives.

4. In each case, the woman sees a solution that would be advantageous to her circumstances, convinces her husband of the benefits, and takes action. In Eve's case, she was directly breaking God's rule. In Sarai's case, there was no prohibition, but there's no indication that it had God's blessing either. Both incidents result in discord, blame-shifting, and a promise of hostility between future generations. Sarai may have thought she was removing an obstacle to the covenant plan by taking things into her own hands, but it actually bears the marks of temptation and human will, not God's will.

5. Hagar seems to be the recipient of God's protection and blessing in this chapter. He seeks her out, encourages her to return to where she will be safe, promises numerous descendants, and speaks to her in quite a personal way. She is being blessed through her connection to Abram—an example of how God's revelation through Abram will bless all peoples of the earth. This incident shows God's concern for the neediest, his ability to see and respond to misery, and his desire to make himself known.

6. God's plan, which includes blessing for Sarai (which she will begin to see in Genesis 18), is much bigger than Sarai's desires and fears. Unlike personal gods of the times, whose roles assumedly revolved around meeting the needs of the individual, God, the ruler of the universe, has a plan which involves all of humanity, and which is centered around his own glory. That's not what you would tell Sarai in the midst of her suffering, nor would you blame her condition on her own actions. But God uses all situations to teach us more about himself and more about ourselves, changing our character to become the people he wants us to be in the process. The same is true today. Christians experiencing hardship are not necessarily dealing with the consequences of "unconfessed sin." They might just be learning some tough lessons according to God's undisclosed plan for them. The good news is that he will never leave or forsake us (Heb. 13:5).

7. Genesis 17:15–22 is the first place where God specifically tells Abraham about Isaac. Abraham was misguided for thirteen years! During that time, the family no doubt poured their love into Ishmael, blessing him through Abram and Sarai. There's no further mention of how Hagar was treated. In the meantime, God safely shields the covenant plan from any further

human tampering since Abram and Sarai think they've done what's necessary on their part.

8. For the first time, God mentions two sides to the covenant agreement: things expected of Abram as well as things God will do for Abram. Right off the bat, Abram is told to walk before God and be blameless. His name change implies unquestioned loyalty to God who has given him a new name and identity. Abraham and his descendants must keep God's covenant, demonstrated specifically by practicing circumcision. God for the first time mentions that Abraham will be the father of many nations, not just one, and that kings will come from him. He establishes the everlasting nature of the covenant, and includes Sarah in the blessing, promising the birth of Isaac.

9. For Americans, nicknames typically signify a close relationship, but actual legal name changes usually only occur with marriage or divorce, signifying a shift in identity from one family to another. Take time to listen to other cultural traditions if they are present in your group. For Abraham, the name change indicates greater understanding of and identity with God's covenant with him. The focus seems to shift from his own privilege in being a father to the promises of the future nations that will come as a result of the covenant. It also signifies Abraham's allegiance to God.

10. Circumcision was a sign of participation in the covenant community. It was an initiation into God's revelatory community and a symbol of subordination to God's plans.[1] Lack of circumcision, accordingly, meant being cut off from the covenant community (17:14). Abraham's immediate response indicates his loyalty and wholehearted desire to identify with God in a covenant community.

11. Sarah laughs when she hears that she and Abraham will have a son in their old age. She sounds pretty dubious, but then tries to cover it up — she certainly doesn't want to jeopardize her chances now by displeasing God's messengers. The steps she took to "help" God's plan are shown up as nothing compared to what God himself will do to advance his plan. Perhaps equally important is her deeper understanding of who God is — nothing is too hard for the Lord. But also, nothing can be hidden from him. Her fears, her unbelief, her laughter — he knows and understands them all, but graciously makes her the mother of nations anyway.

12. Take some time to think about this question. It can be a very helpful review of how God has worked in your life. It can also be very helpful to learn from others if you are in a group.

NOTE

1. Walton, 467.

SESSION 6 LEADER'S NOTES

1. God has made himself known to Abraham more clearly than to other people or nations. Others only know as much about God as they can learn from looking at creation, and incidents such as the Tower of Babel suggest that humanity on its own has not done too well in getting to know God. Abraham's growing knowledge of God is intended to be a blessing to other nations who cannot know him the same way. Once Sodom and Gomorrah are destroyed, Abraham has no means to share the blessing with them.

2. If the cities are spared, the righteous and the wicked will be treated the same way, just as they will if the cities are destroyed. Abraham might be arguing for more time, not for the ultimate safety of the cities. Knowing Lot is living there, Abraham might be hoping that Lot could have a positive influence on that population. Similarly, Abraham could be thinking about his own chances of having an impact on the nations around him as the lone voice of the true God.

3. This seems like a question that you could spend a long time studying. The time of apartheid in South Africa is certainly a negative example of the white minority having a great influence on that society. According to Augustine in *City of God*, the Christian community in Rome had a positive impact on the society around them. Missionaries are a great example of powerful influences for good. More often we can think of individuals who have destroyed cultures and societies by their evil influences. There is definitely power in the hands of a few, which can potentially be used for good or evil. As Christians, we are called to use the power of the gospel to change the world, continuing the mission of Abraham from early on.

4. Lot greets the two angels from the gateway of the city, suggesting that he had probably become a member of Sodom's ruling council.[1] His hospitality matches Abraham's in Genesis 18, and his insistence that the visitors stay with him points to his desire to protect them from the men of the city. Lot takes this protection even further, in trying to defend the angels from the men later, but here his influence fails. He is still considered a foreigner by the Sodomites (19:9), and his efforts of protection are seen as judgmental. When the situation gets out of hand, it is necessary for the angels to save Lot, not vice versa, and he is not taken seriously even by his own sons-in-law.

5. God does not destroy the cities until he has a firsthand account of how bad it is, testifying to his fair administration of justice, but we are told in 18:20 that the outcry is too great to ignore. He does extend a chance to others in the city to escape through Lot (19:12), and takes the initiative to remove Lot and his family when they are hesitating (19:16). He even spares the town of Zoar for Lot's sake. God's mercy is also evident in considering Abraham, who cared for his nephew Lot.

6. The reference in Luke suggests that Lot's wife "looking back" was more than just a glance back at the destruction — it was a wistful wish to return to her old life,[2] which suggests that her destruction was not just an accident. It should make us soberly think about our own end and what is truly precious to us. If our treasure is "things," perhaps we need to think about our priorities. If it's other people, we should waste no time in saying whatever we need to say. No one knows the time of Christ's return or our own deaths, and we need to be ready at any and every moment to greet him with open arms — which also means knowing we are under God's covenant protection through the forgiveness of Jesus Christ.

7. Lot's children are not direct descendants of Abraham, so they are not recipients of the covenant blessing, though they owe their existence to Abraham because of God's mercy on Lot for the sake of Abraham. They are peoples who could be blessed *through* the covenant with Abraham, which should give insight into one reason the Israelites later enter the Promised Land. But, in reality, these nations were at odds with the Israelites for many years.

8. Unlike the last incident (12:10–20), Sarah is fertile this time. God has told her she'll have Isaac within a year. If Abimelech is "allowed near her," Isaac's paternity will be put into question, and the heir of Abraham will again be in doubt. Therefore, God speaks to Abimelech before he could sin against Sarah, and closes the wombs of everyone in Abimelech's household until the issue is resolved.

9. Abimelech may not know anything of God, but he certainly shows respect for right and wrong. Abraham seems to be the one putting the innocent, as well as the covenant, at risk in this case. Just because he is God's chosen instrument does not make him perfect by any means. Because of Abraham, Abimelech learns of God's justice and protection (20:6), his ability

to strike and heal people (20:17 – 18), and his blessing and authority in Abraham's family (21:22 – 23). And because of Abimelech, Abraham is learning what it means to live under God's protection and grace, and how to deal with others with respect.

10. The laughter that sounded somewhat bitter and doubtful in 18:12 has turned into joy and celebration. Sarah has seen God fulfill exactly what he promised — she became pregnant when it seemed impossible in her old age, and bore a son just when God said she would (21:2). God has taken away Sarah's shame and replaced it with laughter. Abraham has been faithful as well, naming Isaac as God told him to, and circumcising him on the eighth day. The covenant is further advanced by the departure of Ishmael, a threat to the covenant from the very beginning.

11. Although God tells Abraham to send Hagar and Ishmael away, he himself watches over them, both in the desert and for the rest of their lives. When Ishmael ("God hears") cries, God hears him and provides water. Ishmael himself becomes the father of twelve nations who live in hostility, all exactly according to God's promises.

12. In one sense, it's encouraging to know that God is bigger than we are, and that he uses us just as we are, complete with blemishes. We don't have to be super-Christians before we can have an impact on the world, since God is the one actually accomplishing his purposes. On the other hand, it's a bit overwhelming to think of the responsibility to make decisions and act in a way that honors him in all we do. It comes as a relief that we are expected to be faithful, not perfect!

NOTES

1. *NIV Study Bible* (Grand Rapids, Mich.: Zondervan, 1985), 33.
2. Walton, 480.

SESSION 7 LEADER'S NOTES

1. Unlike most of the other obstacles to the covenant so far, this one is actually created by God himself and not brought about by a human decision. God wants to test Abraham. Although he is omniscient and knows our hearts, God still regularly asks us to act out our faith and love for him. God wants us to know our hearts, too.

2. Abraham was greatly distressed when he had to send Ishmael away (21:11). Isaac is his only remaining son, the promised son born to Sarah, and Abraham certainly loves him as well (22:2). It would be all the harder to sacrifice him—it made no sense in light of God's promises, and would be incredibly hard for any father to contemplate. To dwell on it for three days with his son walking beside him would no doubt compound his feelings.

3. In God's earlier command, Abraham had something to gain that balanced his loss. In the sacrifice of Isaac there is nothing to gain and everything to lose: his son, the covenant, and all the promises that are based on them. Abraham is being asked to trust God for who he *is* rather than what he has promised, which puts a very high demand on Abraham's faith.

4. Although many of us would be critical of a "health and wealth" gospel, our prayer life often reflects a wish-list of things we're hoping God will provide. Disappointments in life lead many to bitterness, or even to abandoning a relationship with God, rather than to deeper faith. This reflects a misplaced belief that God is there to give us what we want rather than to show us the joy of knowing and trusting him.

5. Thinking this through carefully can help you understand your own heart better. Is it your possessions, the people dear to you, your pride, your background that you treasure? God doesn't necessarily want to take such things away from you, but he might want you to hold on to them with an open hand rather than a closed fist, entrusting things that are precious to you into his care and trusting and loving him regardless of what happens.

6. Abraham was willing to sacrifice his one and only son whom he loved to demonstrate his fear of the Lord. God *did* sacrifice his one and only son whom he loved to demonstrate the extent of his love for us. The things we begin to learn about God through Abraham reach their fullest understanding when we look at Jesus, God's fullest revelation of who he is.

7. In faith, Abraham said that God himself would provide the burnt offering (22:8). He saw how God did that in 22:13, beyond what he could have imagined or planned. The later Israelites hearing this story had many more examples to look back on—leaving Egypt, crossing the Red Sea, living on the food and water that God made available to them. There was growing evidence of God's ability to provide. At Mount Sinai, they saw how God provided a way for them to worship him, even though they were sinful. On this side of the cross, we know that the LORD Who Provides offered his own son as a sacrifice so that we couldn't do for ourselves. There's an incredible freedom that comes with the understanding of God's grace toward us—we are NOT good enough, but Jesus stands in our place, an acceptable offering to God.

8. These names show how big God is—a God so big he can create the universe and sustain all the complexities of it at once, who at the same time is interested in the details of each individual creature. Our God encompasses the extremes of both the cosmic and the personal, which makes him the awesome God who is worthy of our worship. God is fulfilling all the roles of the deities in the ancient world, pointing Abraham to a clearer understanding of who God really is, which is gradually revealed to other nations around as well.

9. God can swear by nothing higher than himself, and by doing so he further strengthens his obligation to keep his covenant. Abraham has now seen God do what he promised to do for twenty-five-plus years, including remarkable things like the destruction of whole cities, a miraculous birth, and providing a sacrifice so that Isaac could live on as the heir of promise. Therefore his word means much more to Abraham now than when he first spoke to him.

10. In 22:17 God adds that Abraham's descendants will take possession of the cities of their enemies. This promise would mean a lot to the later Israelites poised to cross the Jordan River to do just that. It bodes well for their conquest. In 22:18 blessing is connected to obedience, which was integral in the Law given to the Israelites at Mount Sinai.

11. The purchase of land for Sarah's tomb is significant for a couple of reasons—to actually have land in Abraham's name for the first time, and to give future generations a reason to return to Canaan since their ancestors

are buried there. Before Abraham dies, he provides for all his sons, but he clears the way for Isaac to inherit everything he left, the sole heir, consistent with the covenant promise.

12. Abraham and Sarah lived the latter half of their lives learning what it meant to have God with them, living in faith in the midst of the ups and downs that they experienced. As Abimelech pointed out to Abraham in 21:22, "God is with you in everything you do." A blessed life is not defined by circumstances, but by God's guiding presence through it all.

SESSION 8 LEADER'S NOTES

1. The Lord blessed Abraham in every way (24:1) — he has a son, he's in the Promised Land, he has seen God's faithfulness, and he seems quite wealthy. But for the covenant to continue, Isaac must have a wife. Abraham seeks a wife among his own people so that future generations will be distinguishable from the people around him. He sends his servant rather than Isaac so that Isaac remains in the Promised Land.

2. Abraham demonstrates a confidence and trust in God's work. He swears by God as one who is trustworthy. He trusts God to lead him to the right wife for Isaac, rather than trying to manipulate the situation as he did with Hagar. He is confident of God's provision, and he is insistent on Isaac remaining in the Promised Land. This faith in God is passed on to his servant, who sees God's faithfulness when his search for a wife succeeds immediately, causing him to worship the God of Abraham (24:26–27). The servant then spreads an account of God's faithfulness to Abraham's extended family as well (24:33–51).

3. This kind of test essentially puts God in a corner, although he is not obliged to accommodate such a request. Used over the course of history, it has sometimes resulted in false indications of God's will — the sentencing of an innocent person, pursuing actions according to human will rather than truly discerning God's will. It is actually a spiritually immature way to act, although understandable for those times, considering the lack of revelation and understanding of God. Nevertheless, God graciously responds to human weakness at times, in this case showing miraculously his ability to overcome obstacles and clearly fulfill his promises.

4. Signs are really theologically very unsophisticated. It may have been accepted when revelation was still quite new, but is not something we should emulate. Most indicators we look for are not really of the miraculous type, so they are hard to interpret anyway. Now that we have the full revelation of God as well as his Holy Spirit to guide us, we are much better off focusing on our own responsibilities, discerning our own self-will and selfish motivations according to his word to us. God's fingerprints are evident in everyday circumstances if we pray for clear thinking and listen to godly counsel.

5. Rebekah was barren for twenty years; God confirms his covenant blessing with Isaac twice; because of famine Isaac and Rebekah interact with Abimelech in Gerar, when Rebekah masquerades as Isaac's sister; God's blessing on Isaac's crops and flocks causes disputes resulting in them moving around; Isaac reopens the same wells Abraham dug; Isaac and Abimelech make peace treaties. Although Isaac had his struggles, it seems like the second generation is just building on the first, as if it might always be that way.

6. The birth of the twins and the favoritism of the parents introduces a new twist that quickly introduces family conflict, beginning with the birthright incident. Then Esau's marriage to two Hittite women should indicate a red flag that things aren't going to continue quite so smoothly.

7. The original audience would be shocked at Esau's lack of respect for his birthright. However, Jacob is actually the one who makes it an issue, so they are both at fault, even though Esau generally gets more criticism in this section. Esau seems to be ruled by the immediate needs of his stomach here. We begin to see the manipulative nature of Jacob. Neither has the character you would hope to see in someone carrying on and representing God's covenant.

8. Isaac and Rebekah each have their favorite son (25:28), which affects their actions, both in trying to procure Isaac's blessing for their respective favorites, as well as in hiding their actions from each other. Jacob seems to have a tendency toward deception (hence his name) and uses manipulation to get what he wants, regardless of the means. Esau apparently holds grudges, as indicated in 27:36, 41. When it comes down to Isaac's patriarchal blessing, they all succumb to the "sin crouching at their door" rather than doing what is right.

9. Although Isaac's patriarchal blessing is not the same as the covenant blessing, there's a lot of overlap in the language, reflecting Isaac's desire for the blessing to pass on to Esau, not Jacob. This is counter to what God told Rebekah in 25:23, where the older would serve the younger and, if Isaac had been successful in blessing Esau, would certainly contribute to confusion about the covenant blessing and who should serve whom. Rebekah's plotting adds to the family conflict, with the end result that she comes up with the idea to send Jacob out of the country, far away from the Promised Land where he should remain for the covenant's sake. Although not stated

outright, there is no indication that Isaac and Rebekah have planned for an appropriate marriage for either son to prepare for the next generation of the covenant prior to this point. Esau's disrespect for his birthright and his marriage to Hittite women followed by marriage to Ishmael's daughter is certainly counter to the intent of the covenant. His expressed desire to kill Jacob is even more so, particularly as the readers know that Jacob is the true intended heir of the covenant. Jacob's provocation of Esau is a major factor in the family conflict, leading to his deception, Esau's bitterness, and ultimately his departure from the country. It seems like the covenant is hanging by a thread once again because of the human personalities involved.

10. Isaac is convinced that Jacob is Esau, but it almost seems like God must have really befuddled Isaac to make it possible. The hairy arms seem the most convincing, although you'd think someone with poor eyesight would have developed his sense of touch sufficiently to know the difference. He knew the voice of Jacob, but passed over it. He loved the stew, even if it was made from domestic stock, not the wild game that he loved. The smell of the field was the clincher, although the description of the field, like the stew, seems to be more of a domestic nature than the smell Esau would have brought in from hunting. The timing was key, since Esau was right on the heels of Jacob (a reversal of their birth). All in all, the plan seems rather risky and prone to failure.

11. The covenant seems to be back on track in 28:1–9. Isaac has given Jacob his patriarchal blessing, and now adds the covenantal blessing as well. He commands Jacob to marry from Abraham's extended family rather than intermarrying with Hittites. This takes Jacob out of the Promised Land, which is a bit of a risk, but it also removes him from Esau's reach, which was a more immediate threat. Esau's subsequent marriage to an Ishmaelite takes him a step further from the covenant path as well. God has made use of everything — all the family's weaknesses, their actions, timing and perceptions, to accomplish his purposes — he is indeed capable of dealing with all obstacles.

12. God has high expectations for us and holds us accountable for our actions, yet he makes use of our "raw ingredients" to create circumstances and history according to his plan. In his patience, he allows his children to learn and grow over time, although as we've seen in previous chapters, there are

limits to what he will tolerate. There is a point at which we cannot under-stand the mind of God from our finite perspective, which should point us to worship him as we consider his ability to hold all these perspectives in tension as he moves history toward his sovereign purposes.

SESSION 9 LEADER'S NOTES

1. Based on what we've seen of God, there's no doubt that he will bless Jacob and bring him back to the land, protecting him along the way. From Jacob's perspective, however, he has his doubts and seems to be putting conditions on God. The Lord will be Jacob's God only if he follows through on his protection and blessing in the future.

2. Unlike Abraham's servant who had plentiful resources for the bride-price, Jacob has nothing. Through sheer hard work he achieves his goal, but not without difficulty. Jacob the deceiver is deceived by Laban when Leah masquerades as Rachel. Jacob has to work twice as long to get his beloved Rachel, and must take responsibility for Leah as part of the deal.

3. Although Jacob has had interaction with God, he seems a bit distrustful of him and much more confident in his own abilities to get what he wants, whether through manipulation, deception, or plain hard work. God has approached Jacob, but Jacob does not seem to seek our God nor does he acknowledge God's presence in his daily life. This attitude is very prevalent today, where our own hard work becomes our functional theology, although we give lip service to God.

4. The name Reuben means "see, a son!" (but the Hebrew also sounds like "he has seen my misery"); Simeon likely means "one who hears"; Levi sounds similar to the Hebrew "attached"; Judah sounds similar to the Hebrew "praise"; Dan means "he has vindicated"; Naphtali means "my struggle"; Gad means "good fortune"; Asher means "happy"; Issachar sounds like the Hebrew word "reward"; Zebulun likely means "honor"; Joseph means "may he add." Taken in the context of the verses, they reflect the struggles and joys of Leah and Rachel as wives and mothers. Favoritism, both of the wives and of their children, causes conflict in the family. Jealousy over fertility leads to the use of servants as surrogate mothers.

5. You could say that Jacob's actions have come back to bite him! Jacob, who tricked his brother out of his blessing by masquerading as Esau, is tricked into marriage with Leah through her masquerade. Jacob bought the famished Esau's birthright with a bowl of stew. Leah buys a night with Jacob through Reuben's mandrakes, and subsequently gets pregnant with her fifth son. By pilfering Esau's birthright, Jacob's own inheritance is

increased. But through Laban's pilfering of the flocks, Jacob's inheritance is reduced.

6. Our way of life eventually catches up with us. Nothing is hidden from God. Jacob can be out-deceived, but God cannot be out-blessed. With all the trickery that's going on between Laban and Jacob, and the rivalry between Leah and Rachel, God is clearly the one who is in control, choosing to bless Jacob, both with children and livestock.

7. Jacob was urged by his mother to leave Canaan primarily for fear of Esau killing him. He was also commanded by his father to seek a wife from Rebekah's family. He returned partly because of the attitude of Laban and his sons, but primarily because God told him to. He never received any word from Rebekah indicating things were resolved with Esau from twenty years ago, but his family and wealth certainly grew in the meantime.

8. Jacob the deceiver is still involved in deception as he flees Laban's home with all that belongs to him, including his wife Rachel who steals her father's household gods (31:19–21). However, he is also referring to God more than before, listening to him about when to leave, and attributing his blessings to him. When confronted by Laban, Jacob seems to give an honest answer, legitimately defending his work over the past twenty years and acknowledging God's protection and blessing before making a peaceful covenant with his father-in-law. Character change is slow, but it seems at least partial in Jacob.

9. First, Jacob sends messengers to Esau to let him know where he's been, that he's not after any of Esau's goods, and that he's not trying to cause trouble. Second, Jacob prays to God for help. And third, he sends numerous gifts to Esau ahead of his family that would not only emphasize his intentions, but also disrupt any possibility of an ambush by Esau's men. Jacob doesn't know if Esau's four hundred men come in peace or hostility, so he remains fearful and distressed. He has finally reached a point where he's not sure he's capable of caring for his loved ones on his own.

10. Jacob's persistence, boldness, and passion for blessing were present in his early family life, with Laban, and now with God's angel. These are good qualities when used in the right way. But if they're rooted in self-sufficiency and used to lord it over others, they cause more harm than good, as was evident in Jacob's life. In this encounter Jacob submits to God's authority,

as indicated by his name change, thereby letting go of his self-sufficiency and relying on God's sufficiency in his life.

11. Jacob and his family adopt an attitude of servitude toward Esau, and Jacob gives Esau an abundance of gifts, as if returning whatever share of inheritance he may have claimed as his own. These were the components of the birthright and blessing that Jacob could do something about. But the covenant blessing is still firmly established with Jacob, who blesses Esau. With Jacob back in the land with his extensive family, buying land, and setting up an altar in the name of his God, the covenant is doing well once again, thanks to the God who overcomes obstacles.

12. Keep in mind that the journey is very much a process. None of us here has reached the end yet! Just as we saw evidence of process in Jacob, the same is true of us. Thank God he accepts us where we are in life. As a wise professor of mine, David Powlison, often said, it's not how far you've gotten that counts as much as what direction you are facing.

SESSION 10 LEADER'S NOTES

1. At first, Abraham might be amazed at the number of his offspring, but quite likely his amazement would quickly turn to horror at the tactics of his great-grandsons. To make use of circumcision in such a way, and then to act with such violence and greed was not at all characteristic of Abram. His interactions were generally peaceful and respectful of other people in the land, while remaining distinct from them.

2. There is no excuse for the behavior of Shechem or Jacob's sons. If Dinah was consenting to Shechem prior to marriage, there is no excuse for her behavior either. The end does not justify the means. Passions are no excuse for ungodliness. Although intermarriage with Canaanites is temporarily put off, the covenant suffers in its reputation and witness to others. God does not purposely cause evil to happen. Nevertheless, he does use even the sinful as well as the righteous acts of people to his advantage to overcome obstacles.

3. Abraham was circumcised because God commanded him, but he did it out of love, gratitude, and commitment to God. Jacob's sons were motivated by revenge. Shechem was circumcised for love of Dinah—he would do anything for her to be his wife. The rest of the city was motivated by the economic prospects of being in good standing with prosperous Jacob and his family. This seems to get at the core of what each of the characters really wanted in their lives—what their hearts worshiped.

4. As we saw in session 9, Jacob (as his name implied) was a master of deception and manipulation, which was characteristic of the underlying driving force in his life of self-sufficiency. His sons have become experts in the same—deception, coupled with violence or any other means to accomplish their own goals. This was evident in their scheme against Shechem (Gen. 34), in Reuben's actions (35:22), and will continue (Gen. 37–38). God will have to bring about a major change of heart in Jacob's sons to truly turn them to his ways—like Jacob, they will have to abandon deception and learn what it means to truly struggle with the Lord and do what is right.

5. Jacob's family puts aside foreign gods and builds an altar at Bethel. Deborah, Rachel, and Isaac are all buried in the land given to Abraham. God reaffirms his blessing and covenant promises to Jacob; Jacob's last son is

born in the land; and Jacob goes home to the land of Abraham and Isaac. These are all advances for the covenant. However, the daily lifestyle of Jacob's sons, and the fact that they only hid the foreign gods,[1] suggests that all is not well in the hearts of the family. The face we put on in corporate worship does not always reflect what is in our hearts or what is going on in our families. True worship should be reflected in every aspect of our lives, otherwise it suggests that our hearts are still tied up in other things.

6. Just as Jacob's sons were told to get rid of their foreign gods at Shechem, the Israelites in Joshua's time were challenged to make a choice of allegiance—whether to God, the gods of their forefathers, or the gods where they lived before. Every generation is plagued and tempted by other "gods," though they may take on a different appearance at different times. Faith in God is a choice that has to be affirmed anew by every generation. Even though traditions and beliefs can be taught from one generation to the next, true faith is in the heart of the individual and cannot simply be passed down. As the saying goes, "God has no grandchildren."[2]

7. Reuben, Simeon, Levi, and Judah were the first sons born to Leah at a time when the jealousy between Leah and Rachel was intense. Dinah is their full-blooded little sister. Leah sorely felt the lack of love of Jacob, which could have filtered down to her children, particularly the oldest ones. Certainly the favoritism of Jacob for Rachel has passed on to Joseph. It does not seem that surprising, then, that the brothers' anger would be quickly kindled on behalf of Dinah, but against Joseph. Birthright and blessing issues could be factoring into the actions of Joseph's brothers as well, particularly in light of their father's expressed favoritism and Joseph's dreams. Getting Joseph out of the way would clear the way for one of them to inherit the lion's share of their father's wealth and blessing.[2]

8. Reuben has already acted rashly by sleeping with his father's concubine, which could be interpreted as trying to usurp Jacob's inheritance.[3] Saving Joseph could be a last-ditch effort by Reuben to curry favor with his father, to regain his blessing. We know from Jacob's final blessing (49:1–4) that this certainly was an issue.

9. When Joseph was wandering in the fields of Shechem, he was directed to his brothers in Dothan by an unnamed man who encountered him (37:15–17). Finding his brothers was critical to God's plan for Joseph. Had

he not been directed by that stranger, Joseph may have just gone home to his father. Similarly, if the Midianite merchants hadn't come by at just the right time (37:25–28) the story could have ended very differently. In God's providence, seemingly insignificant events can be life-changing in hindsight.

10. To begin with, Judah marries a Canaanite woman. Then he raises such wicked sons that God puts two of them to death. For fear of his youngest son's life, he does not follow through on Levirate law. If it were not for Tamar, the line of Judah would seem to be coming to an end. But perhaps most significant is Judah's interaction with what he thinks is a temple prostitute. In this time and culture, men visited temple prostitutes as a religious ritual, a way of entreating Canaanite gods for a fertile season of crops and flocks. For Judah to be acting this way suggests a shift in allegiance of gods.

11. Tamar masquerades as a temple prostitute. Although that doesn't come off as "good" in our day and age, 38:26 emphasizes the righteousness of the act since she went to such lengths to produce an heir for Judah's family. Deception continues to be used in the family line. This started when Jacob masqueraded as Esau to get Isaac's blessing, then continued when Leah posed as Rachel. Without the masquerade, there may not have been a continuing family line for Jacob or Judah. God can use a crooked stick to accomplish his perfect purposes.

12. Abraham and Isaac both had infertile wives. Jacob and Perez were both second-born twins, so switching around the blessing from birth order was key. Judah would not have been born if Laban hadn't deceived Jacob, nor would Judah have fathered Perez if Tamar hadn't deceived him. These generations all stand in the genealogy of Jesus, the ultimate heir of God's kingdom. This points to (1) God's ability to overcome obstacles, (2) his long-range planning, and (3) his ability to use complicated human dynamics to accomplish his plans.

NOTES

1. Walton, 631.
2. Walton, 668.
3. Walton, 636.

SESSION 11 LEADER'S NOTES

1. Regardless of the circumstances, Abraham and his descendants prospered, particularly when they interacted with other nations. It was clear to everyone involved that God's blessing was following this family, and they often had to move on because of space limitations for all their livestock. In Genesis 39, although the blessing is coming *through* Joseph, it is Potiphar, an Egyptian, who is being blessed. There is a shift in the covenant from establishing the covenant blessing for Abraham's family to bringing the blessing to other nations (see 22:18).

2. Judah created his situation by his choices, including marrying a Canaanite woman. Joseph was forced into slavery by his brothers, but voluntarily fled from Potiphar's wife's advances. Judah's sons were put to death because of their wickedness, while Joseph was experiencing God's blessings in everything he did. Judah seems to be taking things into his own hands, moving away from the God of Abraham as he consorts with what he thinks is a temple prostitute. Joseph submits to God's plans, even slavery, while acting righteously for God's sake. Tamar uses Judah's garments to prove his disobedience to God's ways, while Potiphar's wife uses Joseph's garment to falsely accuse Joseph of trying to use her.

3. Adam and Joseph both had freedom of choice in their actions, despite the fact that Joseph was in slavery. God blessed both of them abundantly. In the face of temptation, however, Joseph displays greater trust and obedience to God than did Adam, and Joseph flees the temptation the woman offers, whereas Adam gave into it. Joseph seems to have grown in his understanding of God, thanks to the covenant, but knowing God does not come automatically, as evidenced by his brothers who had the same spiritual heritage.

4. As 39:21 indicates, God is with Joseph and shows him kindness, even in prison. Joseph is given as much freedom and responsibility as possible within the constraints of prison. God providentially places him in a prison where he has interaction with officials of the court, which ultimately leads him to Pharaoh. On top of that, Joseph is granted understanding of the dreams of Pharaoh's officials, and he was proven right three days later.

5. Joseph still has the dreams from his youth to give him hope (37:5–9), but it takes a lot of trust in God to carry on faithfully in his circumstances, without trying to manipulate things to his own advantage. Without faith, it would be easy to get discouraged or bitter. Knowing how the story ends helps to see the details in a different light. We know Joseph's suffering is temporary—God lifts Joseph out of his dire circumstances to be the second in command in Egypt. We know Joseph's time in Egypt has a purpose—he will save his entire clan when famine hits. Looking at the big picture, Joseph's life is one small piece of redemptive history—Moses is born in Egypt as a result of Joseph's time there, and on the story goes, climaxing in Jesus Christ—an amazing story of love and redemption. We, too, are part of something that God is doing that is bigger than our own lives as he moves all of history to its culmination in Christ (Eph. 1:3–10).

6. Although we're short on details, Joseph must have been a model prisoner in order for the prison warden to give him as much responsibility as he did. Joseph demonstrates care for those assigned to him, as is evident in his interaction with Pharaoh's officials. He takes the initiative to interpret their dreams by consulting God, then he patiently waits when there's nothing more for him to do. God honors Joseph's steps of faith by blessing him in prison, giving him accurate interpretations of the dreams, and eventually using the cupbearer's testimony to secure Joseph's release.

7. The giving and interpreting of dreams is certainly within God's power. More subtly, the inability of the wise men of Egypt to come up with an interpretation, as well as the sudden memory of the cupbearer regarding Joseph, points to God's Spirit prompting their minds as well. On a much grander level, the seven years of abundance and seven years of famine can only be attributed to God. Joseph is given all his abilities by God, but he bears responsibility in accurately interpreting Pharaoh's dreams, coming up with a plan to address the problem, eloquently explaining it to Pharaoh and his officials, and then administering the agricultural economy of Egypt over the next fourteen years.

8. Because in ancient Egyptian culture dreams were an important medium for receiving messages from the gods, God communicated through dreams. He shows the superiority of his revelation over that of the Egyptian wise men

when only Joseph can interpret the dream rightly. Pharaoh recognizes the spirit of God working in Joseph (41:38) and wisely agrees to the plan, trusting in God's man to carry them through. In a way, since the years of plenty come first, Pharaoh has nothing to lose. But the true power of Joseph's God becomes clear in the seven years of famine, an unprecedented crisis for the Egyptians, but happening exactly as Joseph predicted (41:53).

9. In each case—Potiphar's house, the prison, and over Egypt as a whole—Joseph faithfully manages whatever is given to him. And in each case, God blesses him in some way. God's blessing of Joseph is consistent with the promise of Abraham's covenant with God—but here it is extended to Egypt and then to all the surrounding nations when the famine spreads beyond Egypt. However, Joseph's status is significantly different. Although he was respected by his master in each case, Joseph moves from slave to prisoner to Pharaoh's right-hand man, with the dignity that accompanies that position—Pharaoh's signet ring, robes, a gold chain, chariot, and honored proclamation wherever he goes.

10. Joseph is a great example of what it means to reflect God's image. This is most obvious in his high position, but even before that, he performs all his responsibilities with great dignity, earning the respect of everyone around him. He makes use of all that God has given him, accepts even his difficult situations with humility and responsibility, and "rules" the world around him appropriately. He is God's man, used for a time by Pharaoh to accomplish God's purposes.

11. We are not called to imitate every aspect of Joseph's life, but we can certainly learn from his acceptance of circumstances, his recognition of God's hand in all things, and his capacity to reflect God regardless of circumstances. Take time to think how this question applies to your situation personally.

12. God revealed to us his story of relationship with human beings so that we might come to know him better. Using real people to tell the story helps us to understand our own lives as a part of his continuing story. As we see his trustworthiness to others, it gives us hope to believe in his promises now and in the future. It also challenges us to be faithful in whatever our circumstances, and to trust in the salvation he has for his people. Like Abraham earlier, our faith is in a God who can do exactly what he says he will do, because God promises what only he can do.

SESSION 12 LEADER'S NOTES

1. Joseph's dreams that he had when he was seventeen have come true. His brothers are all bowing before him now. Although Joseph doesn't understand everything yet, this is confirmation that God's hand is in all that has happened. Joseph learns that his brothers, including Benjamin, and his father are still well. He also learns that his brothers still struggle with guilt over what they did to him many years ago.

2. Joseph begins by detaining Simeon. Will the brothers abandon another brother to slavery, as they did with Joseph? This is not the ideal test, since Simeon is a son of Leah, not Rachel. But knowing that the famine will continue, Jacob uses Simeon to draw his brothers back to Egypt, bringing Benjamin along with them. By showing favoritism to Benjamin, the other son of Rachel, Joseph tests his brothers further—will they be angry and jealous of him? Joseph sees them up with his own silver cup to make it easy for the other brothers to abandon Benjamin to slavery, just as they did with Joseph. The brothers' reactions show Joseph how their hearts have changed.

3. (a) Joseph, who was accused of spying on his brothers, is now accusing them of being spies. (b) Joseph, who was treated harshly and forcefully held by his brothers, now holds them and treats them harshly. (c) The brothers, who sent Joseph with Midianite traders, now become traders themselves, carrying their brother Benjamin with them. (d) Judah, who came up with the idea to sell Joseph into slavery, offers to become a slave himself rather than allow it to happen to Benjamin. (e) The brothers who deceived their father, breaking his heart, insist on protecting him from further heartbreak.

4. Joseph has consistently been placed in the role of looking out for his brothers (whether they liked it or not). As best we can tell from their words and actions, the brothers have changed, largely because of what they did to Joseph. The repercussions of their wrongdoing seem to have affected them deeply.

5. Joseph sees, and explains to his brothers, how God was the one orchestrating all the events that happened to him. While acknowledging that the brothers are nonetheless responsible for their actions, Joseph explains it

was God who sent him to Egypt to accomplish the greater purpose of providing for Israel and his family in times of famine. What may have been viewed as punishment from a human perspective was really blessing in the bigger picture.

6. Back in Abraham's time, God had already said that his people would be away from their own land for four hundred years. The sojourn in Egypt comes as no surprise to God, but is part of his own plan, which also is clear from the decisive dreams Joseph and Pharaoh had prior to the famine that only God could make happen. God confirms to Jacob in Beersheba that this is a good thing—that it is part of God's nation-building plan, even though it might seem like an odd plan to the people involved.

7. God promises that his presence will be with them in Egypt, that he will continue to build them into a great nation, and he provides abundant land and food for them in Egypt. God continues to deliver on his covenant blessing of food and offspring consistently throughout Genesis. In addition, Israel blesses Egypt (i.e., Pharaoh). The blessing of the nations is demonstrated very concretely here.

8. For the Israelites whom Moses later led out of Egypt, Joseph's life is an encapsulated form of their own lives, except that they have been enslaved for generations. Just as Joseph sees and understands God's purposes for his life for the first time—turning evil to good—the Israelites returning to the Promised Land should gain a better appreciation for God's purposes for them in Egypt, and have hope for their own future as God restores them as he did Joseph.

9. Joseph has virtually absolute control in Egypt through his control of limited resources. The Egyptians are driven to servitude after they sell all their crops and livestock, and are completely dependent on Pharaoh's mercy. But they look to Joseph as having saved their lives during the years of famine. The Israelites acquire property, are fruitful, and increase greatly in number, also saved by Joseph's actions.

10. Jacob takes over Joseph's two children, Ephraim and Manasseh, as his own, leaving to Joseph only any future offspring. In addition, Jacob blesses the younger over the older brother, against Joseph's wishes. For all Joseph's power in Egypt, he is powerless over the covenant blessing. In one sense, Joseph receives a double inheritance, since both his sons receive portions,

but in another sense, he is lost in the reckoning of future generations of Israel. You could almost say that in saving the lives of his people, Joseph lost his own. Joseph's legacy is really in saving this generation of Israelites (and Egyptians), pointing to God's ability to bring good out of evil. The legacy of the covenant is carried on in the name of his sons, rather than his own.

11. The power of guilt and, conversely, the power of forgiveness, are incredible forces in a person's life. As indicated by Joseph's brothers, guilt can still influence attitudes and actions years after an offense is committed. As God told Noah in 9:5, he will demand an accounting of each person for the life of his fellow human beings. Joseph's brothers' reaction shows that such guilt goes deeper than taking the life of a person, since Joseph was not actually killed by their actions. Ultimately, guilt points to the need for a savior. As the author of Hebrews states, even sacrifices fail to fully cleanse people once for all, because people still feel guilty afterward (Heb. 10:1–4). In the end, only Jesus can provide the cleansing power to remove guilt forever (Heb. 10:10). Genesis sets the stage for God to bring good out of the universal evil that permeates all humanity after the fall.

12. God created and established this world and called it good. But it didn't take long for people to rebel against God and come up with ideas for doing things their own way, bringing harm to their relationships with God and with one another. God establishes his covenant with Abraham to reveal his ways more fully, as a way of bringing blessing to all people. It will take longer than the time Genesis tells us about to bring the covenant to full fruition, but the entire book of Genesis reveals God doing just that. God shows himself to be perfectly capable of overcoming all obstacles, providing himself to be good and trustworthy in the process. Although we can't always understand the timing or the means, in spite of everything, God accomplishes what he sets out to do for the glory of his name and the good of his people.

The NIV Application Commentary

Genesis

John H. Walton

Most Bible commentaries take us on a one-way trip from our world to the world of the Bible. But they leave us there, assuming that we can somehow make the return journey on our own. They focus on the original meaning of the passage but don't discuss its contemporary application. The information they offer is valuable—but the job is only half done!

The NIV Application Commentary Series helps bring both halves of the interpretive task together. This unique, award-winning series shows readers how to bring an ancient message into our postmodern context. It explains not only what the Bible meant but also how it speaks powerfully today.

The Bible begins and ends with a revelation of God that gives redemption its basis. From the first verse of Genesis, the book of origins, we encounter a God of personality, character, purpose, and activity. Only in the light of what he shows us of himself as the Creator of our world and the Interactor with human history does the salvation story assume its proper context. Genesis sets things in order: God first, then us.

With characteristic creativity and uncommon depth, John H. Walton demonstrates the timeless relevance of Genesis. Revealing the links between Genesis and our own times, Dr. Walton shows how this mysterious, often baffling book filled with obscure peoples and practices reveals truth to guide our twenty-first-century lives.

Printed Hardcover: 978-0-310-20617-0

Pick up a copy today at your favorite bookstore!

Share Your Thoughts

With the Author: Your comments will be forwarded to the author when you send them to zauthor@zondervan.com.

With Zondervan: Submit your review of this book by writing to zreview@zondervan.com.

Free Online Resources at www.zondervan.com/hello

Zondervan AuthorTracker: Be notified whenever your favorite authors publish new books, go on tour, or post an update about what's happening in their lives.

Daily Bible Verses and Devotions: Enrich your life with daily Bible verses or devotions that help you start every morning focused on God.

Free Email Publications: Sign up for newsletters on fiction, Christian living, church ministry, parenting, and more.

Zondervan Bible Search: Find and compare Bible passages in a variety of translations at www.zondervanbiblesearch.com.

Other Benefits: Register yourself to receive online benefits like coupons and special offers, or to participate in research.

ZONDERVAN
.com®

Lightning Source UK Ltd
Milton Keynes UK
UKHW041233130519

342579UK00006B/340/P

9 780310 276487